I0889531

DANISH VOLUNTEERS OF THE *WAFFEN-SS*

FREIKORPS DANMARK 1941-43

Jens Pank Bjerregaard & Lars Larsen

Helion & Company

Helion & Company Limited
Unit 8 Amherst Business Centre
Budbrooke Road
Warwick
CV34 5WE
England
Tel. 01926 499619
Email: info@helion.co.uk
Website: www.helion.co.uk
X (formerly Twitter): @Helionbooks
Facebook: @HelionBooks
Visit our blog at https://helionbooks.wordpress.com/

Published by Helion & Company 2017. This paperback edition 2025
Designed and typeset by Mach 3 Solutions (www.mach3solutions.co.uk)
Cover designed by Paul Hewitt, Battlefield Design (www.battlefield-design.co.uk)

Text © Jens Pank Bjerregaard & Lars Larsen 2017
Illustrations © as individually credited
Maps drawn by George Anderson © Helion & Company 2017

Every reasonable effort has been made to trace copyright holders and to obtain their permission for the use of copyright material. The author and publisher apologise for any errors or omissions in this work, and would be grateful if notified of any corrections that should be incorporated in future reprints or editions of this book.

ISBN 978-1-804518-43-4

British Library Cataloguing-in-Publication Data.
A catalogue record for this book is available from the British Library.

All rights reserved. No part of this publication may be reproduced, stored in a retrieval system, or transmitted, in any form, or by any means, electronic, mechanical, photocopying, recording or otherwise, without the express written consent of Helion & Company Limited.

For details of other military history titles published by Helion & Company Limited, contact the above address, or visit our website: http://www.helion.co.uk

We always welcome receiving book proposals from prospective authors.

Contents

Preface

When Germany attacked Russia on the 22 June 1941, Denmark broke off its diplomatic connections to Moscow and the Danish government sent its Foreign Minister, Erik Scavenius, to Germany to sign the Anti-Comintern Pact. Back in Denmark Gunnar Larsen, Minister of Transport, and the government believed that giving an exit permit to all officers and volunteers who wanted to join the war on Germany's side would appease the Germans. In that way, it was believed that a more severe German attitude to and occupation of Denmark could be avoided. The Danish government believed that if it said "no" to Danish volunteers, it could entail a major German forcible recruitment of Danish men, not only for the German labour service but for military service as well. Minister of War Soeren Brorsen wrote from the Ministry of War on 8 July 1941: "The Danish government has granted permission to all regular officers of the line, the reserve and conscripts who have been sent home from the Danish Army to freely join *Freikorps Danmark*."

Freikorps Danmark was to be an independent Danish unit and only have Danish officers, as well as Danish being the command language used. However, by September 1941, a German training staff had already arrived, with many German officers and non-commissioned officers. From its beginning, *Freikorps Danmark* was subjected to control by the *Waffen-SS*, which at that time still was subject to the German *Wehrmacht*. Joining the *Waffen-SS* was the only option for foreign volunteers wanting to be admitted into the German Army. After *Freikorps Danmark* had completed its *Waffen-SS* training, it was deployed in one of the harshest places of the Second World War: the Eastern Front.

This book tells the story of *Freikorps Danmark* – in pictures.

We would like to state that this picture book is not trying to glorify the Nazi way of thinking or act as a hero worship of those persons who served in the German Army during the Second World War. Instead, it is intended as a historical picture book about Danes who participated in the war on the side of Germany.

Timeline of *Freikorps Danmark*, 1941-43

1. Establishment of *Freikorps Danmark* – 29/6/1941
2. Langenhorn barracks in Hamburg – 20/7/1941-15/9/1941
3. Treskau barracks in Poland – 16/9/1941-7/5/1942
4. Effort at the Demyansk Pocket in Russia – 7/5/1942-10/8/1942
5. A break from battle – 10/8/1942-8/9/1942
6. On leave of absence in Denmark – 8/9/1942-13/10/1942
7. Redeployment for frontline duty in Russia – 13/10/1942-5/12/1942
8. Winter effort in Velikije Luki in Russia – 5/12/1942-24/3/1943
9. Transport by train to Grafenwöhr in Germany – 24/3/1943-31/3/1943
10. Stay at the barracks in Grafenwöhr – 31/3/1943-20/5/1943
11. *Freikorps Danmark* is abolished in Grafenwöhr – 20/5/1943
12. The Danish volunteers proceeded to the newly-formed *Waffen SS-Regiment 24 Denmark*

Glossary

Anti-Comintern pact: An agreement of 25 November 1936 between Nazi Germany and Japan to fight international communism.

'*Bloddrenge*' (Blood boys): Young Danes who were fully indoctrinated in Adolf Hitler's way of thinking.

Bolshevism: An ideology, which among others builds on the belief that a strong elite should lead the revolutionary change of society.

Bridgehead: Hostile area, typically on the other side of a sea or river.

Cornet: An old term for the lowest rank of officer.

Danish Auxiliary Corps: A Danish military company established on a private initiative in 1919, which consisted of 213 men. The corps joined Estonia in the battles from May to August 1919 during the Estonian War of Independence.

Dog tag: A piece of identification, which could be split in two, one piece staying on the deceased soldier, the second being given to an officer, who had to report the loss.

DNSAP: Danish Nationalist Social Worker Party.

Ehrenblatt des Deutschen Heeres: A major German newspaper of honour during the Second World War.

Envoy: A diplomat with a rank just below ambassador.

'*Folketyskere*': Also known as *Volkdeutsche*, people of German heritage who lived in different enclaves outside Germany prior to 1937, especially in eastern and southern-eastern Europe.

Gestapo: Secret German police.

Motorcycle dispatch rider: Soldiers who carried important messages between companies, usually about the positions of the enemy etc.

NSU: National Socialist Youth.

SD (*Sicherheitsdienst*): Intelligence service.

'*Shellhuset*': The headquarters of the Gestapo in Copenhagen.

The German *Wehrmacht*: Consisted of the army, the navy and the air force. However, it did not include the *Waffen-SS*.

Wochenschau: Produced programmes for cinemas and radio in Germany concerning the war.

1

The Establishment of *Freikorps Danmark* at Langenhorn barracks in Hamburg, 20 July-13 September 1941

This picture book is partly based on photos of eight former *Freikorps Danmark* soldiers. It tells the story of *Freikorps Danmark* in pictures from 1941-43.

The eight former *Freikorps Danmark* soldiers are:

1. Ernst Persson, killed in Russia on 21 January 1944. (Private = the authors).
2. Bernhard Czech, killed in Russia on 29 January 1944. (Private = the authors).
3. Evald Niels Hjalmar Vangebo, survived the war. (Henrik Asferg).
4. Martin Ingemann Bruun Olesen, survived the war. (Jann Hornum).
5. Magnus Moeller, survived the war. (Magnus Moeller).
6. Freddy Boerge Vilhelm Hansen, survived the war. (Poul Christensen).
7. Olaf Jakob Boyesen Friis, survived the war. (Poul Christensen).
8. Knud Per Dahl Nielsen. (Rigborg Dahl Nielsen).

The photos in this picture book have been inserted according to the authors' temporal estimate.

The pictures are all of a variable quality due to age.

Freikorps Danmark is established
Under the command of Lieutenant Colonel C.P. Kryssing
and with Captain Thor Joergensen as chief of staff'

This was a newspaper headline, which the Danish National Socialistic newspaper *Faedrelandet* (*The Homeland*) published on 29 June 1941. Seven days prior to this, Germany had attacked Russia and launched the biggest and bloodiest campaign in the history of the world. With the attack on Russia, Germany was a lot more keen on letting foreign volunteers join German military service. Therefore, the German envoy in Denmark, Cecil Von Renthe Fink, suggested the idea of a new Danish *Finlandskorps* (Finland Corps). The leader of the German *Waffen-SS* recruitment office in Denmark, Eric Lorenz, was afraid that a lot of people who wanted to join as volunteers would not choose the *Waffen-SS* and instead use the new *Finlandskorps*. The leader of the DNSAP (the Danish Nazi Party), Frits Clausen, supported Lorenz, as he was afraid of losing his political influence. However, Finland reported that they no longer admitted foreigners, and put a stop to the idea of a new *Finlandskorps*. The DNSAP and *Waffen-SS* immediately saw the opportunity to establish a new Danish *Freikorps*. On 29 June, the *Waffen-SS* announced the establishment of a *Freikorps Danmark*, after which events moved very quickly. The new commander of *Freikorps Danmark* was the commander of the 5th Artillery Regiment in Holbaek, Lieutenant Colonel C.P. Kryssing. He was not the obvious choice, as at the time he was not a fully convinced Nazi.

The government allows the *Freikorps*

On 2 July 1941, the Danish government decided that Danish officers who wanted to join the new *Freikorps* could withdraw from the Danish armed forces without punishment. At the same time they could, once the war was over, re-enter the Danish Army with the same rank as they had achieved during their German military service. On 3 July, several Danish newspapers reported that the Danish commander of the 5th Artillery Regiment in Holbaek, C.P. Kryssing, with the full support of the Danish government, had been given command of the newly established

Freikorps Danmark. The Minister of War, Soeren Brorson, sent out a circular on 8 July, stating that all Danish officers of the line, the reserve and similar persons could freely join the new *Freikorps Danmark*, and return to the Danish Army once the war was over: which everybody expected to happen very quickly.

The volunteers

The volunteers came from every layer of Danish society, including about 180 who had been a part of the 1,100-strong Finland Battalion from the Winter War of 1939-40. However, there were also others with war experience from other army units, e.g. The French Foreign Legion and the Danish Auxiliary Corps of the Estonian War of Independence in 1919. About 22 percent of those who volunteered for *Freikorps Danmark* were former workers from Germany, and 43 percent of them were members of the DNSAP.

Fædrelandet

FOR·DANMARKS ÆRE·FRIHED·OG·RET

Frikorps „Danmark" er oprettet

Under Kommando af Oberstløjtnant C. P. Kryssing og med Kaptajn Thor Jørgensen som Stabschef

Korpset formeres af Frivillige danske Værnepligtige

Hvervekontoret for Frivillige udsendte i Aftes følgende Bekendtgørelse:

Under Ledelse af Oberstløjtnant C. P. Kryssing, der er Chef for 5. Artilleri Afdeling, Holbæk, er der i Dag oprettet et Frikorps. Frikorpsets Navn er „Danmark".

Stabschef hos Oberstløjtnant Kryssing er Kaptajn i Fodfolket Thor Jørgensen, Holbæk.

Frikorps „Danmark" staar under Kommando af danske Officerer og Underofficerer. Frikorpset formeres af danske Mænd, der har aftjent deres Værnepligt efter 1931.

Alle danske Mænd, som opfylder disse Betingelser, opfordres til at melde sig til Frikorps „Danmark".

Danske Mænd, som ikke opfylder Betingelserne til Frikorps „Danmark", melder sig til Regiment „Nordland". Frikorps „Danmark" og Regiment „Nordland" kæmper for det nye Europas og Danmarks Sag mod Kommunismen.

Kun paa den Maade kan vi blive værdige til at faa vor fulde Frihed

En Udtalelse af Oberstløjtnant C. P. Kryssing

FÆDRELANDET har henvendt sig til Oberstløjtnant C. P. Kryssing og bedt Oberstløjtnanten give Udtryk for sine Bevæggrunde til at stille sig i Spidsen for Frikorps „Danmark".

Oberstløjtnanten udtaler:

— Jeg gaar med i et dansk Korps som et Led af den tyske Hær imod Bolchevikerne, fordi det siden den 9. April er et for haardt Job for mig at være dansk Soldat i Danmark. Jeg har mistet enhver Tillid til, at et demokratisk Danmark kan vække Nationen af den Usselhed, der førte den til den 9. April 1940.

Jeg tror, at danske Soldater, ved at gøre en samlet Indsats mod Bolchevikerne, vil genoprette lidt af den danske Nations Ære.

Jeg tror, at vi kun paa den Maade kan blive værdige til at faa vor Frihed.

Genrejsning af Danmarks Ære ...

Stabschef i Frikorps „Danmark", Kaptajn Thor Jørgensen, udtaler paa „Fædrelandet"s Spørgsmaal om, hvad der har bevæget ham til at gaa med ved Korpsets Dannelse:

— Ved at gaa ind i Kampen mod Bolchevismen og derved støtte Finlands Sag mener jeg, at Tyskland samtidig giver os Chancen for at genrejse Danmarks Ære, der fik et alvorligt Grundskud den 9. April.

NOTER

Til Kamp for et frit germansk Europa

The Danish newspaper *Faedrelandet* in 1941. (Photo: Aarhus Library)

Freikorps Danmark departs

Freikorps Danmark was supposed to be a completely neutral corps regarding politics, but it was subjected to the *Waffen-SS*. The intention was that *Freikorps Danmark* should fight in Danish uniforms, but these were too similar to Russian uniforms. Instead, the German *SS* uniform was chosen. *Freikorps Danmark* was to be led by Danish officers and have the *Dannebrog* as their standard. On Saturday, 19 July 1941, 438 volunteers met at the barracks in Ryvangen. Besides the new recruits, there were also representatives from the DNSAP, as well as Foreign Minister Alex Moerch, who came from the Danish Ministry of Foreign Affairs. The Ministry of War was represented by Colonel Carl Ramsing. Several speeches were given at the barracks, including by C.P. Kryssing, who welcomed the volunteers. After the speeches, all the volunteers marched to Hellerup train station, headed by a German *Luftwaffe* orchestra. They arrived at Hellerup station at 4:00 p.m., where small *Dannebrog* and swastika flags were handed out to those in attendance. While the German orchestra played '*Kong Christian stod ved hoejen mast*' (a well-known old Danish song), the special train left Hellerup station. After a brief stop at Copenhagen Central Station, the train continued through Korsoer, Funen and Jutland on its way towards Hamburg in Germany. On 20 July, the train arrived at Hamburg station, and from there the new recruits marched to Langenhorn barracks, which was located in the northern part of Hamburg. The standard-bearer, a cornet by the name of Mogens Peer Manthey Wagner, marched into the barracks yard, where both Danish and German press were represented.

Langenhorn barracks and oath of allegiance

Langenhorn was an ultra-modern barracks that had been built in 1937-38: it held everything from a dental surgery to a movie theatre. However, the training ground was not ideal, which was a major issue. The four *Freikorps* companies each got their own building, where the volunteers received their new *SS* uniforms. On 5 August, *Freikorps Danmark* was to take an oath of allegiance to Hitler as commander-in-chief of the German *Wehrmacht*. Kryssing, who wore his Danish Knight's Cross for the occasion, made a speech. Erik Knuth, from the Danish General Consulate in Hamburg, was also present. Besides many Danish journalists, there was also the German *Wochenschau*, who filmed the taking of the oath of allegiance. Most of the time at Langenhorn barracks was spent in marches, drills and parades.

Bomb attack, worry and death

On the night of 3 August, *Freikorps Danmark* got its first taste of the war, when planes from the British Royal Air Force bombed the area of the barracks. Two Danish volunteers, Preben Overgaard and Ernst Persson, excelled in extinguishing fires caused by the attack: they both received a letter of thanks from the police president of Hamburg. From the outside, everything seemed fine with *Freikorps Danmark*, but the truth was the total opposite, with the consumption of alcohol particularly high among the officers. The commander, Kryssing, called this to their attention on multiple occasions. On 4 September, the first Danish volunteer died following an incident at the shooting range. The man in question, *Rottenführer* Ejner Hans Poul Nielsen, had wrongly marked the shooting range in the morning, and in the evening, seven of his comrades punished him for it. In the ensuing scuffle, Nielsen sustained a fractured skull when he was struck by the shaft of a bayonet. He was rushed to a camp hospital in Eppendorf, but died later from his injuries. At his funeral on 9 September, a memorial was held for Nielsen, with the four companies of *Freikorps Danmark* gathered together. On 6 September, *Freikorps Danmark* had been told that they should prepare to depart Langenhorn barracks on the 13th, and on the day of departure, the Danish *Dannebrog* flag was taken down for the last time in the barracks yard. All the Danish volunteers in *Freikorps Danmark* were then transferred to Treskau, currently in Poland, by a German freight train. The days of good conditions at Langenhorn barracks were over for the Danish volunteers, and a new period of training awaited in Treskau.

The old gateway to the *Waffen-SS* barracks in Hamburg in 2016. Today, the buildings serve as a hospital. (See page 21 for an old photo from 1941) (Photo: Private)

Opraab fra Kommandanten
for
Frikorps „Danmark".

Danske Mænd!

Med Regeringens Anerkendelse har jeg faaet overdraget Kommandoen over Frikorps „Danmark". — Korpset vil blive sat ind mod den bolchevikiske Verdensfjende, som flere Gange har truet Nordens Sikkerhed og dermed ogsaa vort Fædrelands Frihed og Kultur.

Danske Mænd! Jeg opfordrer Jer til at slutte op i Frikorps „Danmark"s Rækker, for at vi kan gøre en samlet Indsats mod Bolchevismen.

Danske Soldater, som har aftjent eller aftjener deres Værnepligt, kan uden Hensyn til Vaabenart indrulleres i Korpset.

For Danmarks Ære, for vort Folks Frihed og vort Fædrelands Fremtid slutter vi os sammen i Vaabenbroderskab med de Nationer, der allerede er traadt an til Kamp mod Europas og dermed ogsaa mod vort Lands Fjende.

C. P. Kryssing,
Oberstløjtnant, Kommandant for
Frikorps „Danmark".

Hvervekontorer over hele Landet.
Hovedkontor: Rosenvængets Allé 32 - København Ø.
Kontorerne er aabne i Dag Søndag.

Proclamation from C.P. Kryssing, the commander. "Join *Freikorps Danmark*!" (Photo: Private)

INDMELDELSESSKEMA

for Krigsfrivillige til Waffen-SS og Frikorps „Danmark"

Familienavn: .... Fornavn: ....

Født den: .... Fødested: ....

Bopæl: .... Gade og Husnummer: ....

Stilling: .... Straffet: Ja, Nej

Jeg er af arisk Afstamning. Gift: Ja, Nej Børn: ....

Har tjent i den danske Hær fra .... til ....

Jeg forpligter mig for Krigstid, 4 Aar eller 12 Aar

(Hvad der ikke passer, bedes streget!)

...., den ....

(Underskrift)

Klip her

BESTEMMELSER

vedrørende de Paarørendes Underholdssatser og andre Ydelser, der kommer til Anvendelse i Danmark.

1. Underhold for Paarørende

Fra og med den 1. Juni 1942 at regne, fastsættes der følgende Skema- og Underholdssatser:

a) Skemasatser for Hustruer:
Ved en Nettoindtægt hhv. tilsvarende

Nettoindtægt af indkaldte indtil	udgør Skemasatsen:
Kr. 400.—	Kr. 175.00
Kr. 450.—	Kr. 185.00
Kr. 500.—	Kr. 200.00
Kr. 550.—	Kr. 215.00
Kr. 600.—	Kr. 230.00
Kr. 650.—	Kr. 255.00
Kr. 700.—	Kr. 280.00
Kr. 750.—	Kr. 305.00
Kr. 800.—	Kr. 330.00
Kr. 850.—	Kr. 355.00
Kr. 900.—	Kr. 380.00
Kr. 950.—	Kr. 405.00
Kr. 1000.—	Kr. 435.00
over 1000.— Kr.	Kr. 465.00

b) Underholdsbidrag for:

I. Familieunderholdsberettigede, der er fyldt 16 Aar og er Familieforsørgere (f. Eks. en af Forældrene af Indkaldte) eller som Enkeltperson fører en egen Husholdning Kr. 120.00.

II. Andre underholdsberettigede Medlemmer af Husholdningen over 16 Aar, (f. Eks. den anden Forældrepart eller den Indkaldtes Børn, der er fyldt 16 Aar) Kr. 55.00.

III. Underholdsberettigede under 16 Aar, som lever i den Indkaldtes Husholdning, hos dennes Hustru eller hos Slægtninge i lige Linie (for Eks. de i den Indkaldtes Husholdning levende Børn indenfor Ægteskabet) Kr. 50.00. 2. Barn Kr. 55.00. 3. Barn Kr. 60.00. 4. Barn Kr. 65.00, fra og med 5. Barn Kr. 70.00. For Børn udenfor eller før Ægteskabet betales de paa Grundlag af skriftlige Krav fra Kommunerne fordrede Underholdssatser.

IV. Underholdsberettigede under 16 Aar, som ikke lever i den Indkaldtes Husholdning, hos dennes Hustru eller hos Slægtninge i lige Linie Kr. 85.00.

2. Regelmæssige Understøttelser

a) I Huslejehjælp ydes det fulde Beløb af den virkelige Husleje. Bebor den Underholdsberettigede en Lejlighed i en Ejendom, som tilhører den Indkaldte eller den Underholdsberettigede, saa ydes en Huslejehjælp i Højde med de stedlige, sædvanlige Lejetakster for denne Lejlighed.
b) Sygekassebidrag.
c) Forsikringspræmie incl. Krigsrisikopræmie.
d) Fagforeningsbidrag.
e) Skatter.
f) For Brændsel betales indtil 350.— Kr. aarlig.
g) Studiegæld, efter nærmere Aftale

3. Særhjælp, kun een Gang

a) Ved Fødsel af et Barn Kr. 200.00, desuden Læge, Jordemoder og Plejeomkostninger.
b) Udgifter ved Besøg af saarede Ægtefæller eller Sønner.
c) Udgifter for Land — eller Rekreationsophold for trængende, børnerige Familier.

4. Regelmæssige Understøttelser for Afbetalingsforpligtelse i begrænset Omfang

5. Driftsunderstøttelser,

hvis der ikke betales Familieunderhold:

a) Løn til Stedfortræder iflg. forelagt Lønkvittering.
b) Lejeunderstøttelse for Forretningslokaler.

6. Til ugifte Frivillige

ydes en regelmæssig Hjælp af Kr. 45.—, hvis de tilhører Wehrsoldgruppen 16, og Kr. 55.—, hvis de tilhører Wehrsoldgruppen 15, saafremt der ikke stilles Anmodning om Familieunderhold efter Afsnit B, Punkt 2—4, ved Opfyldelse af de fornødne Forudsætninger til Familieunderhold.

C/0974

A Danish registration form for *Freikorps Danmark* from 1941. (Photo: Private)

C.P. Kryssing made a recruitment speech lasting half an hour on '*Statsradiofonien*' (Public Broadcasting Service) on 9 July 1941. (Photo: Jann Hornum)

Danish volunteer soldiers who had followed the recommendation. (Photo: National Museum)

The future *Freikorps Danmark* soldiers ready for departure. (Photo: Private)

The recruits marched to Hellerup train station on 19 July 1941. (Photo: Private)

A German *Luftwaffe* orchestra leading the marching volunteers from the barracks of Ryvangen to Hellerup train station. (Photo: Private)

People 'heiled' their farewells to the future *Freikorps Danmark* soldiers. (Photo: Private)

The train with the volunteers heading for Hamburg in Germany. (Photo: Henrik Asferg)

The new soldiers painted Nazi phrases on the train for Hamburg. (Photo: Private)

On the right commandor C.P. Kryssing arriving at Hamburg (Photo: Jann Hornum)

Recruits and officers of *Freikorps Danmark* marched from the train station in Hamburg to Langenhorn barracks. In the centre, Mogens Peer Manthey Wagner carries the *Dannebrog*. He died in Russia in January 1944. On the left is Chresten Madsen Brodersen, who fell in the Demyansk Pocket in 1942. On the right is the former Finland volunteer Johannes Just Nielsen, who was also killed in the Demyansk Pocket. (Photo: Private)

Freikorps Danmark marches through the gateway to Langenhorn barracks on 20 July 1941. (Photo: Private)

The gateway to Langenhorn barracks in Hamburg, 1941. (Photo: Henrik Asferg)

The same place in 2016. (Photo: Private)

Langenhorn barracks in 1941. (Photo: Henrik Asferg)

The Danish volunteers in *Freikorps Danmark* were to be trained to become frontline soldiers. The barracks had good billeting conditions, but exercise facilities were lacking. (Photo: Henrik Asferg)

Langenhorn barracks in 1941. (Photo: Henrik Asferg)

Langenhorn barracks in 1941. (Photo: Henrik Asferg)

Olaf Jakob Boyesen Friis, a *Freikorps Danmark* soldier, at the horse stables. (Photo: Poul Christensen)

Volunteer Evald Niels Hjalmar Vangebo in his new *SS* uniform. (Photo: Henrik Asferg)

SS-Gruppenführer Hans Jüttner and C.P. Kryssing at the oath of allegiance. (Photo: Henrik Asferg)

The parade at the oath of allegiance. (Photo: Henrik Asferg)

The oath that the volunteers swore: "I swear by god this holy oath that I in the battle against Bolshevism will offer the supreme commander of the German *Wehrmacht* unconditioned obedience that I as a brave soldier at all times am ready to sacrifice my life to keep this oath." (Photo: Henrik Asferg)

A Danish volunteer, Broder Henry Jensen, brings forth the Danish flag. It is uncertain where and when the picture was taken. (Photo: Henrik Asferg)

The *Dannebrog* was brought forward at the oath of allegiance. To the left is Christian Von Eggers, in the middle Hans Ulrik Petersen and to the right Johannes Hellmers. (Photo: Private)

Freikorps Danmark marches to a funeral parade. (Photo: Henrik Asferg)

The funeral parade was for *Rottenführer* Ejner Hans Poul Nielsen. (Photo: Henrik Asferg)

A group of *Freikorps Danmark* soldiers. (Photo: Poul Christensen)

Volunteer soldiers of *Freikorps Danmark* in their new *SS* uniforms. (Photo: Henrik Asferg)

The weapons had to be cleaned, inspected and oiled. Second from the right is Knud Oluf Pedersen, who was killed on 2 June 1942 at Biakowo in the Demyansk Pocket. (Photo: Henrik Asferg)

Three unknown officers. (Photo: Poul Christensen)

A group of officers pose for the cameraman. (Photo: Henrik Asferg)

The field kitchen, which was set up in the barracks yard. (Photo: Henrik Asferg)

2

Treskau barracks in Poland 16 September 1941-7 May 1942

The whole of *Freikorps Danmark* arrived at Treskau on 16 September 1941. As opposed to Langenhorn, the barracks were old and rundown. On the other hand, the area was almost perfect for drills and training for the soldiers: being on the other side of the River Warthe, it was ideal for them to practise with their 80mm mortars.

The barracks in Treskau

The barracks of *Freikorps Danmark* was originally an old convent from the twelfth century, which had been transformed into a psychiatric hospital in 1838. When the Germans entered Poland in 1939, most of the patients at the hospital were executed or sent to concentration camps. After this, the Germans converted the buildings into a huge military barracks. C.P. Kryssing, the commander of *Freikorps Danmark*, had his own house at the barracks, while the rest of the Headquarters Company was installed in nearby buildings. The houses of the officers enjoyed good conditions, such as a casino, officer's mess etc. The first four companies were all in the main building, while the 5th Company (the Replacement Company) was installed in the neighbouring town of Rothsand.

The problems continue

Despite *Freikorps Danmark* arriving at a place with almost ideal conditions for its training, the internal problems had followed it from Langenhorn. The biggest problem was the alcohol consumption among officers. Several of them were intoxicated in the morning for drills, and a general lack of discipline started to spread among the privates in the form of bad hygiene, military attire and poor or even no saluting of officers. As their training started, some volunteers wanted to get out of their contracts. Several soldiers did not return to Treskau after their leave of absence. The majority of those who stayed away were quickly arrested and sent back to the barracks. Some of the arrested were sentenced to jail: however, this would only be served when the war was over. A single person, Hans Hermann Valdemar Jensen, stood out. He did not return after his leave of absence, and during this time he had abused a girl. For this, Jensen was arrested and sentenced to death. The sentence was carried out on 2 June 1942 in Treskau, where he was executed by firing squad.

Broken deal

In September 1941, the Danish government sent 60 trucks, 60 cars and 70 motorcycles to *Freikorps Danmark* in Treskau. The original plan was that the corps should be ready for front-line duty on 15 February 1942. However, this was not possible, as *Freikorps Danmark* was far from fully trained. Due to this lack of training, a German training staff was brought in. This was not well received by the commander, Kryssing, who regarded it as a breach of the agreement that only Danish officers should train *Freikorps Danmark*. At the same time, the Germans would make *Freikorps Danmark* much more political. In December 1941, Ejner Joergensen and Steen Andersen, both from the DNSAP, arrived at Treskau to talk to the volunteers. The corps had split into two groups; one supported a more National Socialistic approach to their training, while the other was against this.

Despite these internal problems, Christmas Eve of 1941 was celebrated with a grand party featuring a Christmas tree and proper Christmas food, and each volunteer got half a bottle of wine and 24 cigarettes.

New commander

During December 1941, the Germans had started to search for a new commander for *Freikorps Danmark*. In particular, they were getting tired of the many internal problems in the unit, as well as C.P. Kryssing's dissatisfaction with the arrival of the German training staff. Kryssing and some of his officers were under pressure, not only from the Germans, but also from some of the corps. In particular, it was the more convinced National Socialists who pressed to depose Kryssing. On 23 February 1942, Kryssing along with 14 officers of his staff were deposed and transferred to other German units. Only three days later, the new commander arrived: the former guardsman and commander of the 2nd Company in *Den Danske Finlands Bataljon* (The Danish Finland Battalion) from 1939-40, C.F. von Schalburg, who came from the *SS-division Wiking*.

New times

Discipline and training improved after the arrival of von Schalburg. At the same time, *Freikorps Danmark* rapidly became more National Socialistic. Von Schalburg was a completely different commander and personality to Kryssing. Among other things, he partook equally in the training of the private soldiers and held special 'comrade' evenings for the volunteers. The German choice of von Schalburg as the new commander was not a random one. In terms of propaganda, he was a good draw for *Freikorps Danmark*, and was a relatively well-known name within National Socialist groups in Denmark.

The old convent/hospital/*SS* barracks for *Freikorps Danmark* in Treskau, Poland, is just an empty ruin today. (Photo: Private)

Departure to the front

On 7 May 1942, at 2:00 a.m., the alarm went off at the barracks. It was a day which the soldiers in *Freikorps Danmark* had looked forward to for a long while: the departure to the front. At 7:00 a.m., they left Treskau for the airfield in Heiligenberg, and on 7 and 8 May, the corps was flown by German aircraft to the city of Demyansk in Russia. The *Freikorps* motorcycle dispatch riders remained in Treskau, as they were to depart to the Russian front by train about 14 days later.

Leif Lund, a *Freikorps Danmark* volunteer, in front of the *SS* stone at the entrance to Treskau barracks. The inscription on the stone reads: "My honour is called loyalty" (*Meine Ehre Heisst Treue*). (Photo: Henrik Asferg)

The entrance to the barracks in Treskau. (Photo: Henrik Asferg)

Weapon drill in the barracks yard. (Photo: Henrik Asferg)

Soldiers of *Freikorps Danmark* training in the barracks yard. (Photo: Henrik Asferg)

Freikorps Danmark in the barracks yard. (Photo: Henrik Asferg)

Freikorps Danmark at a weapon tutorial in the barracks yard. (Photo: Henrik Asferg)

Freikorps Danmark at the exercise yard. (Photo: Henrik Asferg)

Three unknown soldiers of *Freikorps Danmark*. (Photo: Jann Hornum)

A group of soldiers of *Freikorps Danmark* in the country. (Photo: Private)

The field kitchen at the shooting range. (Photo: Henrik Asferg)

Firing practise in the country. (Photo: Henrik Asferg)

Lunchbreak for the soldiers at the shooting range. (Photo: Henrik Asferg)

Hakon Elander, on the left, with two unknown comrades. (Photo: Henrik Asferg)

A group of soldiers of *Freikorps Danmark* at the shooting range. (Photo: Private)

Three unknown soldiers of *Freikorps Danmark* relax in the countryside. (Photo: Henrik Asferg)

Training in accurate shooting. (Photo: Private)

Soldiers of *Freikorps Danmark* marching across a bridge. (Photo: Jann Hornum)

Kaj Nielsen, left, and Evald Hansen. (Photo: Henrik Asferg)

A group of volunteer soldiers of *Freikorps Danmark*. (Photo: Henrik Asferg)

Soldiers of *Freikorps Danmark* attract the curiosity of a young boy. (Photo: Magnus Moeller)

Two *Freikorps Danmark* soldiers examine orders. (Photo: Private)

Training in the use of a mortar. (Photo: Rigborg Dahl Nielsen)

Group photo of *Freikorps Danmark* soldiers in the field. Top right is Martin Ingemann Bruun Olesen. (Photo: Jann Hornum)

Freikorps soldiers training with boats at the River Warthe. (Photo: Poul Christensen)

Soldiers of *Freikorps Danmark* crossing the River Warthe with a barge during training. (Photo: Henrik Asferg)

Freikorps Danmark soldiers in a small boat on the River Warthe. (Photo: Henrik Asferg)

Soldiers of *Freikorps Danmark* landing at the River Warthe. (Photo: Henrik Asferg)

Training with machine guns. (Photo: Jann Hornum)

Hans Fischer, a soldier of *Freikorps Danmark*. (Photo: Private)

Shooting exercise in the area in front of the barracks. (Photo: Henrik Asferg)

Shooting exercise and getting familiar with the weapons. (Photo: Henrik Asferg)

Training with machine guns in the field. (Photo: Henrik Asferg)

Training with machine guns in the snow. (Photo: Henrik Asferg)

Shooting exercise in front of the barracks. (Photo: Henrik Asferg)

Soldiers of *Freikorps Danmark* huddle to keep warm around a fire. (Photo: Jann Hornum)

Ejner Joergensen, on the left, from DNSAP, greets a soldier of *Freikorps Danmark*. (Photo: Private)

The closet and bed of a soldier of *Freikorps Danmark* at the barracks. (Photo: Henrik Asferg)

A soldier of *Freikorps Danmark* posing in the dining hall at the barracks. (Photo: Private)

The barracks decorated for Christmas. (Photo: Henrik Asferg)

Celebrating Christmas Eve. (Photo: Poul Christensen)

Johannes Jensen, right, and two unknown soldiers at a bridge. (Photo: Henrik Asferg)

Many made clear they were unhappy with the first commander, C.P. Kryssing. (Photo: Henrik Asferg)

After the criticism, C.F. von Schalburg replaced C.P. Kryssing. (Photo: Henrik Asferg)

Taking part in a medical exercise. (Photo: Henrik Asferg)

Medical exercise. (Photo: Henrik Asferg)

Two unknown soldiers in the forest. (Photo: Henrik Asferg)

Magnus Moeller, a soldier of *Freikorps Danmark*, poses in the snow. (Photo: Magnus Moeller)

Bernhard Czech, a soldier of *Freikorps Danmark*. (Photo: Private)

A photograph believed to show *Freikorps Danmark* troops in the city of Poznan, Poland. (Photo: Henrik Asferg)

Two motorcycle dispatch riders in the forest. (Photo: Jann Hornum)

Kaj Mogens Krogh served as a motorcycle dispatch rider. (Photo: Henrik Asferg)

A group of soldiers of *Freikorps Danmark* at the River Warthe. (Photo: Poul Christensen)

C.F. von Schalburg arrives as the new commander of *Freikorps Danmark*. (Photo: Rigborg Dahl Nielsen)

C.F. von Schalburg inside the Treskau barracks for an inspection. (Photo: Private)

From the right: Boy Hansen (German), C.F. von Schalburg and K.B. Martinsen (Photo: Private)

In the centre are, from the left, K.B. Martinsen, C.F. von Schalburg and Boy Hansen (German). (Photo: Private)

Scharführer Anton Kern (German, left), with an unknown *Hauptscharführer*. (Photo: Rigborg Dahl Nielsen)

Enjoying a meal from the back of a truck are, from the left, Hans C. Nordholm, W. Christensen and Karl Eduard Wahle. (Photo: Private)

Training with machine guns in the forest. (Photo: Henrik Asferg)

Untersturmführer Karl Eduard Wahle (left), a German, who died on 25 May 1942 in Biakowo, Russia, with *Untersturmführer* Andersen. (Photo: Rigborg Dahl Nielsen)

Two unknown soldiers of *Freikorps Danmark* at the road sign to the village of Mienkowo about 5km from Treskau. (Photo: Henrik Asferg)

The dentist of *Freikorps Danmark*, Ernst Müller, with his wife. (Photo: Private)

A group of *Freikorps Danmark* soldiers changing the tyre of a truck. (Photo: Private)

Practical exercise in how to rescue a wounded/dead soldier. (Photo: Jann Hornum)

C.F. von Schalburg, the commander, participating in a field exercise. (Photo: Private)

C.F. von Schalburg, the *Freikorps* commander, takes part in a field exercise. (Photo: Private)

A group of soldiers of *Freikorps Danmark* on their way to a field exercise. (Photo: Private)

Soldiers of *Freikorps Danmark* during training. (Photo: Poul Christensen)

Soldiers of *Freikorps Danmark* at the barracks. (Photo: Henrik Asferg)

Soldiers at a railway station on their way back to Treskau, Easter 1942. (Photo: Private)

Taking a break during a field exercise. (Photo: Jann Hornum)

Soldiers developed skills during field exercises. (Photo: Poul Christensen)

Six unknown soldiers of *Freikorps Danmark*. (Photo: Henrik Asferg)

Freikorps Danmark soldiers during a field exercise. (Photo: Poul Christensen)

Members of *Freikorps Danmark* with an officer during a field exercise. (Photo: Poul Christensen)

Soldiers help free a vehicle from the mud at the side of a track. (Photo: Private)

Two unknown soldiers of *Freikorps Danmark* take a break. (Photo: Jann Hornum)

Eating a meal from the field kitchen. (Photo: Henrik Asferg)

A group of soldiers of *Freikorps Danmark* training in the forest. (Photo: Henrik Asferg)

Field kitchens kept the troops fed. (Photo: Henrik Asferg)

A group of soldiers of *Freikorps Danmark* inspect a motorcycle. (Photo: Jann Hornum)

Three unknown volunteer soldiers of *Freikorps Danmark*. (Photo: Poul Christensen)

Olaf Jakob Boyesen Friis. (Photo: Poul Christensen)

This *Freikorps Danmark* soldier is named on the back of the picture as *Sturmmann* Soerensen. (Photo: Rigborg Dahl Nielsen)

Two *Freikorps* soldiers take part in a training exercise. Knud Per Dahl Nielsen, top, was killed in Narva, Estonia, on 13 February 1944, while Aage Kjaerulf, below, fell the same year in Witino, Russia, on 21 January. (Photo: Rigborg Dahl Nielsen)

A soldier takes cover during military training. (Photo: Rigborg Dahl Nielsen)

Soldiers learned how to make use of natural and man-made cover during training sessions. (Photo: Rigborg Dahl Nielsen)

Military training also involved bayonet practise. (Photo: Rigborg Dahl Nielsen)

Four *Freikorps Danmark* soldiers taking aim during military training. (Photo: Rigborg Dahl Nielsen)

Live firing with rifles and machine pistols during military training. (Photo: Rigborg Dahl Nielsen)

A soldier firing what appears to be an MP38 or MP40 machine pistol during a training exercise. (Photo: Rigborg Dahl Nielsen)

A group of Danish medical soldiers. (Photo: Henrik Asferg)

Motorcycles and trucks ready for departure to the Russian Front. (Photo: Private)

Vehicles ready for transportation to the Eastern Front. (Photo: Private)

Vehicles of *Freikorps Danmark* lined up in front of the barracks. (Photo: Private)

Soldiers of *Freikorps Danmark* with trucks ready for departure to the Eastern Front. (Photo: Private)

Part of *Freikorps Danmark*'s fleet of transport. (Photo: Private)

Part of the corps' field kitchen, ready to go to the Eastern Front in Russia. (Photo: Rigborg Dahl Nielsen)

Freikorps Danmark drive from the barracks to the train station in trucks. (Photo: Private)

The train is packed with men and material, ready for departure. Note the Danish flag raised on the side of the train. (Photo: Rigborg Dahl Nielsen)

3

The Demyansk Pocket in Russia 7 May-10 August 1942

Soldiers of *Freikorps Danmark* were flown to the airfield in the town of Demyansk in Russia by Junkers *Ju-52* planes on 8 and 9 May 1942. A sight of wrecked tanks and cars met the Danish volunteers, along with a city in ruins. For the majority of the Danish volunteers, this was their first experience of the great destruction of modern war. They were quartered among the civilian population in small villages near the town of Losnitzy: the 1st Company in Ignatizy, 2nd Company in Werezina, 3rd Company along with the staff in Zemena and 4th Company in Podboresje. The motorcycle dispatch riders arrived by train through Staraja Russa to join *Freikorps Danmark* at the front on 11 June.

Background

On 22 June 1941, when Germany launched its attack on Russia, codenamed 'Barbarossa', the Russian armed forces quickly retreated. However, the German offensive came to a halt in late 1941 and early 1942. On 8 January 1942, the Russians surprised the Germans with a counteroffensive. A month later, after intense battles, the Russians succeeded in trapping six German divisions, about 95,000 men, in an area the size of Funen (a Danish island). This was the Demyansk Pocket, and the only option for the Germans was to supply the trapped soldiers by air. About 180 German planes containing ammunition, food and other necessities (carrying a total of about 300 tons) flew each day to keep the trapped German soldiers supplied. The situation was untenable for the Germans, and Operation *Brückenschlag* was launched. German forces would attack the Russians from outside the pocket, while the trapped Germans also attacked the Russians at the same time. The plan was to breach the Russian circle, and 73 days later a corridor had been made to the trapped German forces around the towns of Biakowo and Vasilevschina. Holding this corridor was vital for the Germans, as it was the only land route in and out of the Demyansk Pocket. The area which *Freikorps Danmark* had to defend was part of the corridor in and out of the Demyansk Pocket. This area consisted of mud, swamp and birch and spruce forest. The German pioneer troops had made a road consisting of crossed logs, called the '*Rullebanen*' (roadway), which went 90km from the town of Staraja Russa to Demyansk. Primarily, *Freikorps Danmark* was to defend the section between the towns of Vasilevschina and Biakowo. In small groups, soldiers of *Freikorps Danmark* carried out patrols in the nearby muddy forests. On 17 May, the first Danish volunteer died: *Oberscharführer* Orla W. Jensen stepped on a mine. He had previously served in the Danish armed forces as well as the French Foreign Legion. The first major battle of *Freikorps Danmark* took place on 20 May, when Russian forces tried to capture the town of Biakowo. During the following days, many soldiers were killed in clashes, among them the first officer of *Freikorps Danmark* to fall, *Untersturmführer* Hans Carl Nordholm, who died from severe injuries. The Russians crossed the Robja stream in late May, about 5km west of Biakowo, and established a large bridgehead at the village of Ssutoki.

The commander falls

Freikorps Danmark was assigned to *Totenkopf*, a German *SS* division. *Standartenführer* Hellmuth Becker, the commander-in-chief, wanted to move the whole front line, so it would be easier for German artillery to target the Russians. However, this order served no meaningful purpose, and made the positions of *Freikorps Danmark* even more vulnerable. On 2 June, the *Freikorps* launched an attack on the Russian bridgehead. The positions were successfully captured, but shortly thereafter, Russian artillery bombed the area, while German artillery also bombed it by mistake. The commander of *Freikorps Danmark*, C.F. von Schalburg, launched another attack, but was killed after stepping on a mine and subsequently being hit by a bomb from a Russian mortar. After this, the Danes withdrew to their original position: they had lost 32 killed, among them their commander, and about 100 wounded. The fallen were buried at the *Freikorps Danmark* cemetery in Biakowo on the following day.

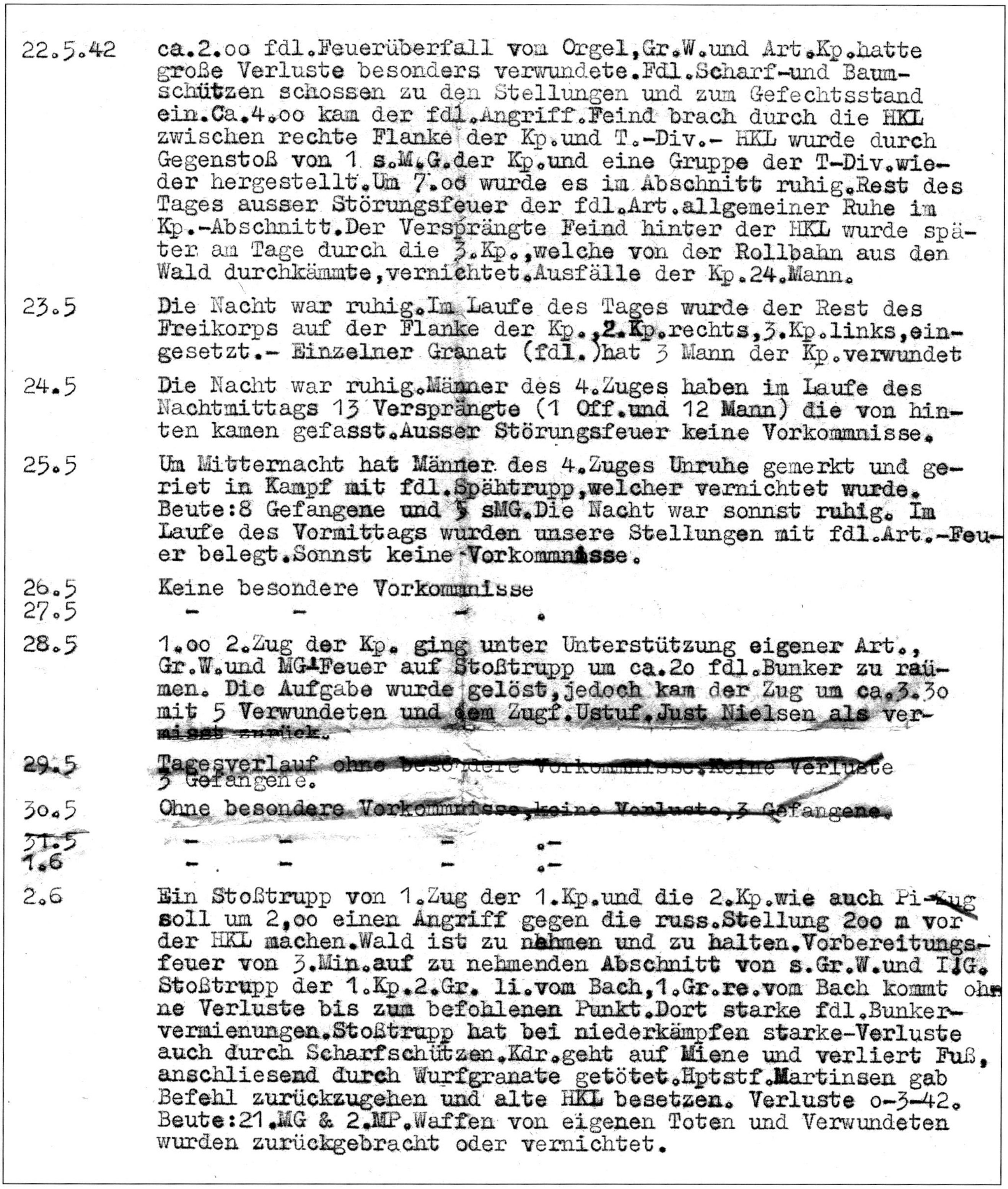

22.5.42 ca.2.oo fdl.Feuerüberfall von Orgel,Gr.W.und Art.Kp.hatte große Verluste besonders verwundete.Fdl.Scharf-und Baumschützen schossen zu den Stellungen und zum Gefechtsstand ein.Ca.4.oo kam der fdl.Angriff.Feind brach durch die HKL zwischen rechte Flanke der Kp.und T.-Div.- HKL wurde durch Gegenstoß von 1 s.M.G.der Kp.und eine Gruppe der T-Div.wieder hergestellt.Um 7.oo wurde es im Abschnitt ruhig.Rest des Tages ausser Störungsfeuer der fdl.Art.allgemeiner Ruhe im Kp.-Abschnitt.Der Versprängte Feind hinter der HKL wurde später am Tage durch die 3.Kp.,welche von der Rollbahn aus den Wald durchkämmte,vernichtet.Ausfälle der Kp.24.Mann.

23.5 Die Nacht war ruhig.Im Laufe des Tages wurde der Rest des Freikorps auf der Flanke der Kp.,2.Kp.rechts,3.Kp.links,eingesetzt.- Einzelner Granat (fdl.)hat 3 Mann der Kp.verwundet

24.5 Die Nacht war ruhig.Männer des 4.Zuges haben im Laufe des Nachtmittags 13 Versprängte (1 Off.und 12 Mann) die von hinten kamen gefasst.Ausser Störungsfeuer keine Vorkommnisse.

25.5 Um Mitternacht hat Männer des 4.Zuges Unruhe gemerkt und geriet in Kampf mit fdl.Spähtrupp,welcher vernichtet wurde. Beute:8 Gefangene und 5 sMG.Die Nacht war sonnst ruhig. Im Laufe des Vormittags wurden unsere Stellungen mit fdl.Art.-Feuer belegt.Sonnst keine Vorkommnisse.

26.5 Keine besondere Vorkommnisse

27.5 - - - .

28.5 1.oo 2.Zug der Kp. ging unter Unterstützung eigener Art., Gr.W.und MG-Feuer auf Stoßtrupp um ca.2o fdl.Bunker zu raümen. Die Aufgabe wurde gelöst,jedoch kam der Zug um ca.3.3o mit 5 Verwundeten und dem Zugf.Ustuf.Just Nielsen als vermisst zurück.

29.5 Tagesverlauf ohne besondere Vorkommnisse,keine Verluste 3 Gefangene.

30.5 Ohne besondere Vorkommnisse,keine Verluste,3 Gefangene.

31.5 - - - .-

1.6 - - - .-

2.6 Ein Stoßtrupp von 1.Zug der 1.Kp.und die 2.Kp.wie auch Pi-Zug soll um 2,oo einen Angriff gegen die russ.Stellung 2oo m vor der HKL machen.Wald ist zu nehmen und zu halten.Vorbereitungsfeuer von 3.Min.auf zu nehmenden Abschnitt von s.Gr.W.und I.G. Stoßtrupp der 1.Kp.2.Gr. li.vom Bach,1.Gr.re.vom Bach kommt ohne Verluste bis zum befohlenen Punkt.Dort starke fdl.Bunkervermienungen.Stoßtrupp hat bei niederkämpfen starke-Verluste auch durch Scharfschützen.Kdr.geht auf Miene und verliert Fuß, anschliesend durch Wurfgranate getötet.Hptstf.Martinsen gab Befehl zurückzugehen und alte HKL besetzen. Verluste o-3-42. Beute:21.MG & 2.MP.Waffen von eigenen Toten und Verwundeten wurden zurückgebracht oder vernichtet.

The war journal of Per Soerensen, commander of 1st Company, covers the events on 2 June 1942, when C.F. von Schalburg was killed in combat. The German text in the final paragraph includes the detail that: "The commander stepped on a mine and lost a foot, and was subsequently killed by a mortar bomb. *Hauptsturmführer* Martinsen ordered a retreat to the old main frontline. Casualties and wounded 0-3-42 [1st Company lost no officers killed, three privates killed and 42 wounded]. Loot: 21 machine guns and 2 sub-machine guns, from our own dead or wounded, were brought back or destroyed." (Photo: Private)

The village of Bol. Dubowizy

North of the town of Vasilevschina was the village of Bol. Dubowizy, which was one of the few places in the area where the ground was dry, meaning tanks could be used. The Russians occupied the village, and therefore it was a major threat for a Russian breakthrough at the '*Rullebanen*'. On 5 June, *Freikorps Danmark*, supported by *SS-Division Totenkopf* and other units of the *Wehrmacht*, launched an attack on the village. Fourteen hours later, Bol. Dubowizy was captured. However, eight soldiers of the corps were killed during this action. On the night of 6 June, the Danes were relieved of their positions at Bol. Dubowizy. *Sturmbannführer* Hans Albert von Lettow Vorbeck, their new commander, arrived on 9 June. Late on 10 June, Russian forces attacked Bol. Dubowizy and quickly recaptured the village. The following day, *Freikorps Danmark* was deployed and once again launched an attack on Bol. Dubowizy. The attack failed, and the village was never recaptured. *Freikorps Danmark* lost 23 men, among them Vorbeck, the new commander, as well as two company commanders, Boy Hansen of 2nd Company and Alfred Nielsen of 3rd Company. After this, K.B. Martinsen was appointed as commander of *Freikorps Danmark*. Until 17 July, the front was relatively quiet, with only minor actions and losses. However, on 17 July, the Russians launched a major offensive to capture the town of Vasilevschina and close the important supply route to the Demyansk Pocket. However, the attack failed. On 4 August, when *Freikorps Danmark* was taken out of the front line, it had suffered 121 killed, five missing and about 300 wounded in combat. Many later died of their injuries. On 10 August, the Danish volunteers left the Demyansk Pocket by freight train. Later that day, they arrived at Mitau in Latvia, where they stayed until their leave of absence in Denmark.

Life at the front

The Danish volunteers suffered from filthy and primitive conditions. They lived in damp bunkers, which were often filled with water from the swamp, causing diseases, particularly of the skin. Mosquitos and lice were almost as great enemies as the Russians: the mosquitos carried diseases such as typhus. Another major health risk was the high number of rotting corpses which were strewn around the area, especially in shell and water holes. The Danes could not avoid being acquainted with the numerous Russian prisoners of war. Many Russians surrendered, but their fate is unknown. There are examples of many being shot, while others were transported to one of the major prison camps, *Arme gefangenen sammenstelle Nr. 14*, which was situated in the Demyansk area. Many of the Russian prisoners of war were renegades. Some of these became part of *Freikorps Danmark*, Sofus and Piotr being the best-known. They both became a sort of mascot of *Freikorps Danmark*, and they followed the Danish volunteers to the last battles in Berlin in 1945. After that, their fate is unknown.

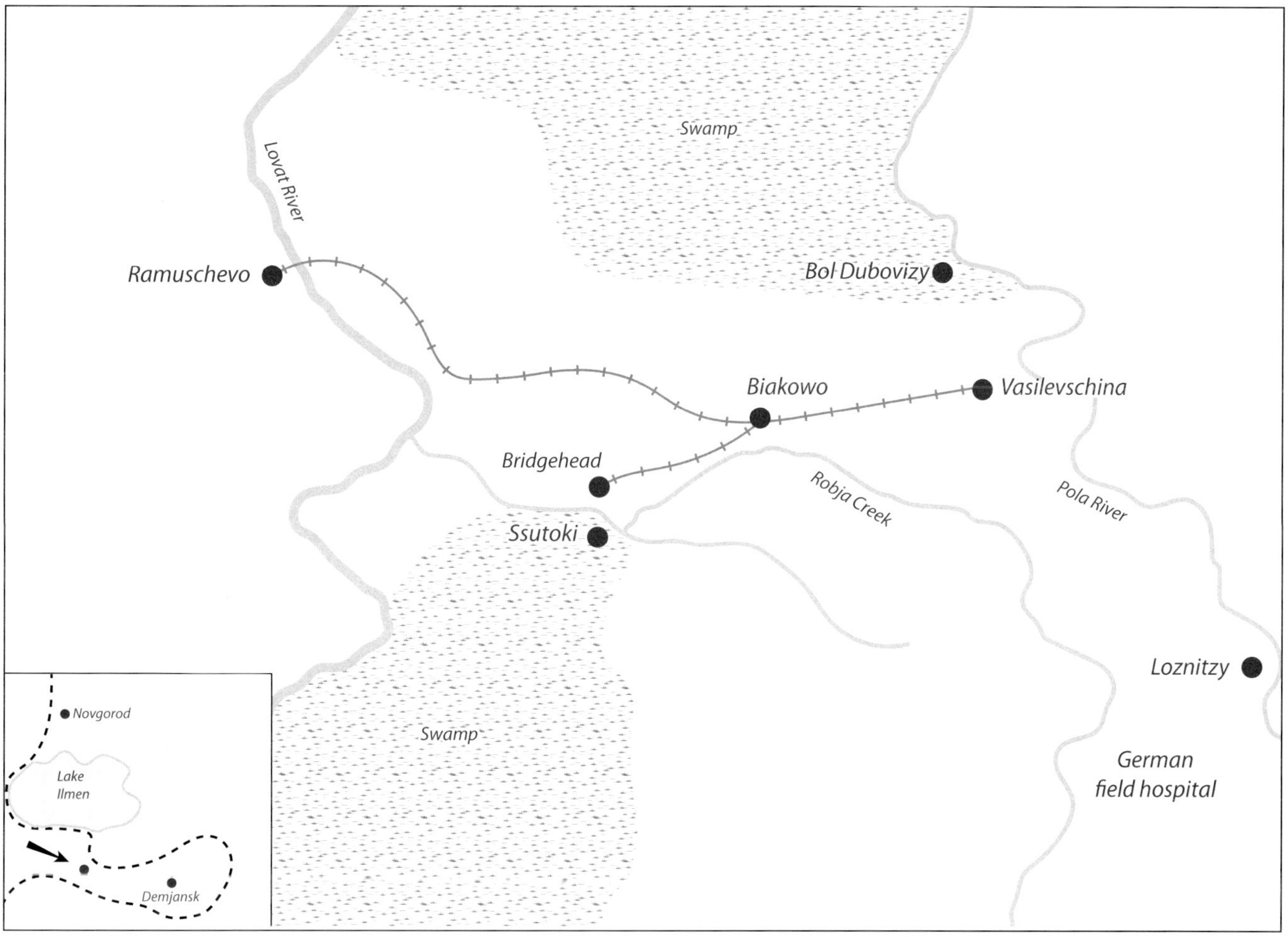

A map of *Freikorps Danmark*'s area of battle in summer 1942. (Map by George Anderson)

The airfield in Heiligenberg. (Photo: Jann Hornum)

Preparing to embark at the airfield in Heiligenberg. (Photo: Jann Hornum)

Freikorps Danmark soldiers gather at the airfield in Heiligenberg. (Photo: Private)

Another shot of the airfield in Heiligenberg. (Photo: Private)

The cabin of a *Ju-52*. (Photo: Private)

Approaching the town of Demyansk. (Photo: Jann Hornum)

Aircraft get ready to land at Demyansk. (Photo: Private)

A *Ju-52*, which landed safely on the landing strip in Demyansk. (Photo: Private)

The wreck of a car that had been destroyed during the fighting. (Photo: Private)

This is thought to be a picture of the devastated town of Staraja Russa. (Photo: Private)

This is most likely another picture of the town of Staraja Russa, north of the Demyansk Pocket. (Photo: Private)

Another picture believed to be of Staraja Russa. (Photo: Private)

Bombed out buildings in Staraja Russa. (Photo: Private)

The wreck of a truck. (Photo: Private)

A soldier of *Freikorps Danmark* with a destroyed Russian T34-76 tank. (Photo: Private)

Not all casualties in the Pocket were human. (Photo: Private)

Soldiers inspect a destroyed Russian KV-1 tank. (Photo: Poul Christensen)

A destroyed Russian tank, most likely at Bol. Dubowizy. (Photo: Poul Christensen)

A stockpile of what is believed to be German anti-tank mines. (Photo: Jann Hornum)

A German truck destroyed on the *'Rullebanen'*. (Photo: Jann Hornum)

destroyed Russian KV-1 tank (note the additional bolt-on armour). The text on the memorial tablet reads: "Three unknown German comrades." (Photo: Jann Hornum)

Hans Olsen Müller on top of a destroyed Russian T34-76 tank. (Photo: Jann Hornum)

Soldiers of *Freikorps Danmark* inspect a destroyed Russian T34-76 tank. (Photo: Jann Hornum)

A soldier of *Freikorps Danmark* with a destroyed and burnt-out Russian KV-1 tank. (Photo: Jann Hornum)

A soldier of *Freikorps Danmark* with destroyed enemy T-26 tanks. (Photo: Private)

A light German half-tracked motorcycle. (*SdKfz 2, Kettenkrad*). (Photo: Private)

A group of soldiers in front of '*Solbakken*'. (The Sun Hill), the house which served as their quarters. (Photo: Jann Hornum)

A Russian farmer.
(Photo: Jann Hornum)

A Russian family of farmers with two children. (Photo: Jann Hornum)

A Russian farmer with his horse and carriage. (Photo: Jann Hornum)

Two Russian women with a small child. (Photo: Private)

A Russian farming family. (Photo: Private)

A soldier of *Freikorps Danmark* with his Russian host family. (Photo: Private)

A group of soldiers of *Freikorps Danmark* at the house they were quartered in. (Photo: Private)

A soldier of *Freikorps Danmark* photographed with a small Russian boy. (Photo: Poul Christensen)

Afterwards, they shared his field ration. (Photo: Poul Christensen)

This is most likely the main street in Bol. Dubowizy. (Photo: Private)

Soldiers of *Freikorps Danmark* in front of a Russian house. (Photo: Private)

Some Russian farmers ploughing the earth. (Photo: Private)

A group of soldiers of *Freikorps Danmark* at a house, which was their quarters. (Photo: Private)

Some Russian women in front of '*Villa Frygtlos*' (The Fearless Villa). (Photo: Private)

A truck that was wrecked on the '*Rullebanen*'. (Photo: Jann Hornum)

Vehicles suffered from many problems on the '*Rullebanen*'. (Photo: Poul Christensen)

A stretch of the '*Rullebanen*' running through a forest. (Photo: Private)

Horse-drawn and vehicular traffic battle through the '*Rullebanen*' mud. (Photo: Private)

There was a lot of mud along the '*Rullebanen*'. (Photo: Private)

The wooden '*Rullebanen*' seen from the inside of a truck. (Photo: Private)

The Russians often targeted and destroyed parts of the '*Rullebanen*'. (Photo: Private)

In many places, the '*Rullebanen*' was impassable. (Photo: Poul Christensen)

A camouflaged German *SD. Kfz 232* armoured car on the '*Rullebanen*'. (Photo: Private)

Russians prisoners working to repair the '*Rullebanen*'. (Photo: Private)

Unknown soldiers of *Freikorps Danmark* in the mud on the '*Rullebanen*'. (Photo: Jann Hornum)

A German half-tracked vehicle being used as a rescue vehicle. (Photo: Poul Christensen)

Horses being rescued after falling in the mud. (Photo: Private)

A half-tracked vehicle towing trucks free of the mud on the '*Rullebanen*'. (Photo: Magnus Moeller)

Freikorps Danmark vehicles pause along the '*Rullebanen*'. (Photo: Jann Hornum)

Even motorcycles struggled in the '*Rullebanen*' mud. (Photo: Jann Hornum)

A 'guesthouse' on the '*Rullebanen*'. (Photo: Private)

Wrecked vehicles littered the '*Rullebanen*'. (Photo: Jann Hornum)

Russian prisoners are lined up for the camera. (Photo: Jann Hornum)

Many Russian prisoners were injured. (Photo: Jann Hornum)

Prisoners of war carrying wounded and dead soldiers. (Photo: Jann Hornum)

Prisoners of war transporting war materials. (Photo: Jann Hornum)

Another shot of prisoners of war transporting wounded and dead soldiers. (Photo: Jann Hornum)

Large numbers of Russian prisoners were taken. (Photo: Jann Hornum)

Piotr, a Russian prisoner of war, was enrolled in *Freikorps Danmark*. (Photo: Private)

Russian prisoners are allowed a brief rest on their march into captivity. (Photo: Private)

Prisoners of war building the '*Rullebanen*'. (Photo: Private)

Some Russian prisoners even managed a smile for the camera. (Photo: Private)

Oberscharführer O.W. Jensen was the first Dane of *Freikorps Danmark* to fall on the Eastern Front. (Photo: Jann Hornum)

Soldiers pause to pay their respects at the cemetery. (Photo: Private)

Helmets of the fallen were left over their graves. (Photo: Private)

Anorther view of the cemetery. (Photo: Private)

The grave of *Schütze* Erik Jensen. (Photo: Magnus Moeller)

The grave of *Sturmann* Johannes Bratvig. (Photo: Private)

The grave of *Obersturmführer* C.M. Brodersen. (Photo: Private)

The grave of *Schütze* Niels M. Nielsen. (Photo: Private)

Some of the many graves of the fallen. (Photo: Private)

On the left is K.B. Martinsen. On the right is Eduard Hein, a German, who was killed in January 1944. (Photo: Private)

The last photo taken of C.F. von Schalburg before he was killed on 2 June 1942. (Photo: Private)

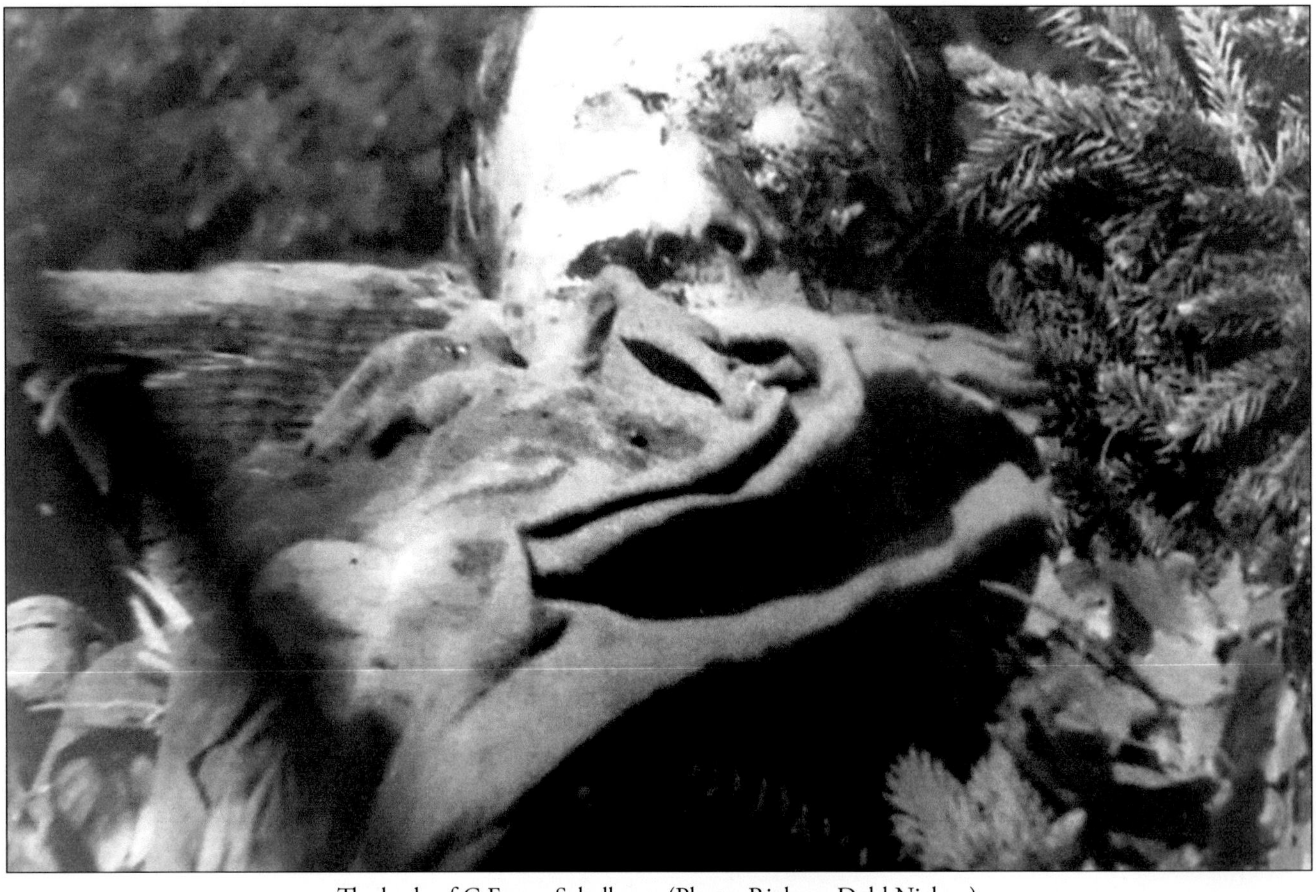

The body of C.F. von Schalburg. (Photo: Rigborg Dahl Nielsen)

The body is taken to its final resting place (Photo: Private)

Eight soldiers carry the body to the grave. (Photo: Private)

A guard of honour prepares to fire a volley at von Schalburg's graveside. (Photo: Private)

The body is ready to be lowered into the grave. (Photo: Private)

A simple grave for the commander of *Freikorps Danmark*. (Photo: Private)

Per Soerensen (left) and Erling Iversen in the Demyansk Pocket. (Photo: Private)

Verner Bircow Lassen, right, nicknamed 'Balbo', makes a gruesome discovery. (Photo: Private)

Among *Freikorps Danmark* members are Hans Olsen Müller (third from left) and Erik Herloev Nielsen (on the right). (Photo: Jann Hornum)

A group of unknown soldiers of *Freikorps Danmark* during a lull in the fighting. (Photo: Jann Hornum)

A bivouac erected by soldiers of *Freikorps Danmark*. (Photo: Jann Hornum)

Freikorps soldiers pause while building a bunker in the forest. (Photo: Jann Hornum)

Building bunkers in the forest. (Photo: Jann Hornum)

A well camouflaged completed bunker in the forest offered protection for several soldiers. (Photo. Jann Hornum)

Another well camouflaged bunker in the forest. (Photo: Private)

A soldier of *Freikorps Danmark* emerges from an earth bunker with a bottle of wine. (Photo: Private)

Soldiers use a chainsaw to saw logs for their bunkers. (Photo: Jann Hornum)

The field kitchen at work at Biakowo. (Photo: Jann Hornum)

Sailing on the streams of Robja. (Photo: Jann Hornum)

Two *Freikorps* soldiers in a dinghy on the streams of Robja. (Photo: Private)

Sailing in a dinghy on the streams of Robja. (Photo: Private)

More sturdy boats were used for sailing on the River Lovat. (Photo: Jann Hornum)

The ferry crossing at the River Lovat. (Photo: Jann Hornum)

An unknown Danish soldier looks to the skies. (Photo: Jann Hornum)

Soldiers of *Freikorps Danmark* giving each other haircuts. (Photo: Jann Hornum)

Soldiers eating from a field kitchen at the front. (Photo: Private)

Hans Olsen Müller, who was born on 12 May 1911 and died in 1980. As a former police officer, he inspected the new Danish recruits for any criminal past. If they had a record, they were discharged from *Freikorps Danmark*. On 18 May 1945, Müller was arrested and sentenced to eight years in prison. (Photo: Jann Hornum)

Soldiers of *Freikorps Danmark* relaxing in a ditch while smoking pipes. (Photo: Jann Hornum)

Relaxing during a lull in the fighting are Eduard Hein (left), Per Soerensen (centre) and P. Neergaard-Jacobsen. (Photo: Jan Hornum)

Unknown soldiers relax by a motorcycle. (Photo: Jann Hornum)

Three unknown soldiers of *Freikorps Danmark*. (Photo: Jann Hornum)

Freikorps soldiers Hans Olsen Müller (left) and Erik Herloev Nielsen. (Photo: Jann Hornum)

Food was transported to the frontline by horse and carriage. (Photo: Jann Hornum)

A motorcycle and sidecar crossing the river at what is believed to be the village of Ramushevo. (Photo: Private)

Commander K.B. Martinsen shares a bottle with some of his men. (Photo: Jann Hornum)

Freikorps Danmark soldiers learning about weapons at the front. (Photo: Jann Hornum)

Erik Lorentzen at a Russian crossroads. (Photo: Private)

Per Soerensen, commander of 1st Company, takes time out to relax. (Photo: Jann Hornum)

Unknown soldiers in the mud on the '*Rullebanen*'. (Photo: Jann Hornum)

Soldiers of *Freikorps Danmark* in front of their bunker, which they had named 'Julia'. (Photo: Jann Hornum)

Freikorps Danmark men rest up between battles. (Photo: Jann Hornum)

Per Soerensen (second from the left) with C.F. von Schalburg and other officers. (Photo: Private)

An unknown soldier of *Freikorps Danmark* with an artillery shell. (Photo: Poul Christensen)

Some soldiers start building a bunker. (Photo: Private)

Receiving post from the family. (Photo: Private)

A camouflaged German *Leichte Feldhaubitz* 10.5cm howitzer. (Photo: Private)

A group of soldiers with protection against mosquitos. (Photo: Jann Hornum)

Soldiers of *Freikorps Danmark* sitting with a young Russian boy. (Photo: Poul Christensen)

Freikorps Danmark soldier Martin Ingemann Bruun Olesen. (Photo: Jann Hornum)

A medical bunker at Biakowo. (Photo: Private)

Two soldiers reading the Danish newspaper *Faedrelandet*. (Photo: Jann Hornum)

Erik Herloev Nielsen (right) reading the Danish newspaper *Faedrelandet*. (Photo: Private)

The field kitchen on a truck. (Photo: Poul Christensen)

A soldier takes a rest. He is wearing the Iron Cross on his uniform. (Photo: Jann Hornum)

A group of unknown *Freikorps Danmark* soldiers in the forest. (Photo: Jann Hornum)

Two unknown soldiers of *Freikorps Danmark*. (Photo: Poul Christensen)

On the left with a pipe is Niels K. Jensen, who was killed on 11 July 1942. (Photo: Private)

Soldiers practise how to use a gas mask. (Photo: Private)

A truck pulling an anti-aircraft gun. (Photo: Jann Hornum)

Soldiers of *Freikorps Danmark* in what is thought to be the town of Biakowo. (Photo: Private)

A soldier of *Freikorps Danmark* outside his bunker. (Photo: Poul Christensen)

Difficut conditions in the swamps where *Freikorps Danmark* fought. (Photo: Private)

Soldiers of *Freikorps Danmark* at a frontline toilet. (Photo: Private)

Passing through a burning village are Kai Burchardt (right), Felix Sejer (centre) and Svend Aage Jensen. (Photo: Bogans forlag)

O.H. Larsen was captured and maltreated by the Russians. (Photo: Private)

Resting in the woods are Poul Windekilde Hansen (right) and Jens Andreas Kristensen (centre) with an unknown comrade. (Photo: Private)

On the right is Leon Langebaek, holding a machine pistol, next to an unknown soldier. (Photo: Private)

Relaxing and sunbathing while reading a newspaper is Verner Bircow Lassen (right) next to an unknown soldier. (Photo: Private)

The war often seemed many miles away: Adam Andersen (right) sunbathes with an unknown soldier. (Photo: Private)

Verner Bircow Lassen with a 50mm Russian mortar shell. (Photo: Private)

A group of soldiers of *Freikorps Danmark* wearing forage caps. (Photo: Private)

War photographer Flemming Helweg Larsen (left) with K.B. Martinsen. (Photo: Private)

Jarl Steenbach (left) and war photographer Flemming Helweg Larsen (centre) with an unknown comrade. (Photo: Private)

Members of *Freikorps Danmark* at what is believed to be the town of Biakowo. (Photo: Private)

A stockpile of logs, used to build the '*Rullebanen*'. (Photo: Private)

Freikorps Danmark on their way home from the front on leave. (Photo: Private)

Materiel being loaded on the train which would carry the *Freikorps* away from the Pocket. (Photo: Private)

Vehicles of *Freikorps Danmark* being prepared for departure. (Photo: Private)

Vehicles and other materiel are loaded onto a train which would take the *Freikorps* away from the Pocket. (Photo: Private)

Commander of 1st Company, Per Soerensen (wearing cap), waits by the side of a railway track. (Photo: Private)

To the right is the commander of *Freikorps Danmark*, K.B. Martinsen, with other officers. (Photo: Private)

At the station in Tuleblia: a Russian prisoner of war, whom the *Freikorps* brought with them. (Photo: Jann Hornum)

Commander of 1st Company, Per Soerensen, ready for departure. (Photo: Private)

Soldiers of *Freikorps Danmark* aboard a freight train. (Photo: Jann Hornum)

Freikorps Danmark soldiers appear happy to be leaving the front in a freight train. (Photo: Jann Hornum)

Freikorps Danmark vehicles safely embarked ready for departure from the front. (Photo: Private)

Erik Steen Jensen, on the truck, ready to leave the Pocket. He was killed at Narva in Estonia in 1944. (Photo: Private)

Music being played on the train by *Freikorps* members happy to be leaving the front. (Photo: Bogans forlag)

The trained stopped so that soldiers could get fresh milk from a cow. (Photo: Bogans forlag)

Bernhard Czech, a soldier of *Freikorps Danmark*, looks forward to his return home. (Photo: Private)

Two unknown soldiers of *Freikorps Danmark*. (Photo: Private)

An unknown soldier of *Freikorps Danmark* is happy to be leaving the front line. (Photo: Private)

Den tyske Fører dekorerer danske Frivillige

93 Officerer, Underofficerer og Menige i Frikorps Danmark er blevet udmærket med Jernkorset for tapper Kamp mod den bolchevikiske Fjende

Fra Partifører Frits Clausen har FÆDRELANDET modtaget følgende Liste over Officerer, Underofficerer og Menige i Frikorps Danmark som for Tapperhed i Kampen mod den bolchevikiske Fjende i den tyske Fører og Øverstbefalendes Navn er blevet dekoreret med Jernkorset af General i Waffen SS og SS Obergruppenführer Eicke:

Ustuf. Dürkop, Werner, 1. og 2. Klasse
Hstuf. Martinsen, Knud Børge, 1. Klasse
Rtf. Nielsen, K. P. D.
Sch. Nielsen, Kaj W.
Sch. Mikkelsen, C. R. B.
Rtf. Petersen, C. A. F.
Sch. Andersen, O. R. F.
Sch. Fikmann, A. N. I. L.
Str. Skjødsholm, N. P.
Rtf. Nørskov, J. J.
Ostuf. Hansen, Boy
Ustuf. Dombek, Josef
Obschaf. Høgg, Willi
Untch. Kling, Fritz
Str. Christensen, M. M.
Str. Langschwager, Hermann
Sch. Ratzen, H.
Untch. Pedersen, Carlo
Schtz. Enna, Kay
Strm. Nielsen, E. Herløv
Strm. Jørgensen, Christian
Scht. Christensen, Gunner
Str. Espersen, Peter
Untch. Jensen, Erik Steen
Obch. Jørgensen, Jørgen
Hstuf. Martinsen, Knud Børge
Scht. Claudi, Christ. A.
Scht. Schrøder, Karl
Scht. Schmidt, Leif
Scht. Schuchardt, Siegfried
Obcha. Graabeck, Axel
Scht. Jepsen, Lauritz
Scht. Hansen, Frede
Scht. Jørgensen, Gunner
Scht. Jensen, Niels Konrad
Scht. Jensen, Chr. Rommy
Scht. Gaade, Børge Marius
Untch. Harlund, Hugo
Ostuf. Brodersen, Christian
Ustuf. Henneke, Heinz
Ustuf. Fenger, Erik Vagn
Ustuf. Nielsen, Alfred
Usk. Szimanski, Julian Stef
Rtf. Nielsen, Frederik
Str. Reinke, Paul
Scht. Thomsen, Hans Jens
Ustuf. Kure, Ole Peter

Usha. Puschtla, Konrad
Scht. Broder, Günthers
Scht. Henker, Paul
Unshf. Nielsen, Johannes Just
Obsh. Kern, Anton
Untch. Beck, Ole
Untch. Westergaard, Erik
Strm. Nielsen, Helge Broch
Scht. Nielsen, Niels Steffen
Scht. Larsen, Verner Rodo
Scht. Madsen, Svend Erik
Scht. Jensen, Kaj Arthur
Scht. Jonassen, Oswald
Scht. Hansen, Anthon Nissen
Scht. Jensen, Lauritz
Scht. Friedemann, Jonny
Scht. Normann, Alfred Oscar
Scht. Hermansen, Holger K.
Scht. Ankersen, Ewald F. Chr.
Scht. Nybo, Niels
Scht. Nielsen, Hans T.
Scht. Rasmussen, Verner
Andersen, Per
Christensen, J.
Ostuf. Sørensen, Per
Ustuf. Andersen, H. P. K.
Oscha. Madsen, L. A.
Rtf. Nissen, Hans Chr.
Rtf. Andersen, Hans Chr.
Rtf. Nielsen, Aage Ishej
Ustuf. Paulsen, Egil
Oscha. Park, Arni Ejner
Rtf. Schmidt, Iver
Strm. Schmidt, Heinrich
Strm. Karlssen, Hjalmar
Oscht. Thorgilsen, Paul
Ostuf. Hein, Eduard
Ustuf. Lohe, Konrad, Dr.
Str. Friis, Asmus
Ustuf. Müller, Hans
Usha. Zillmann, Fred
Unsh. Schubert, Kurt
Strm. Klages, Heinrich
Strm. Sbresny, Gustav
Strm. Gelscinnus, Erich
Osch. Staschert, Wolfgang

A list of the Danes who received the German Iron Cross.

Vaaben SS har meddelt FÆDRELANDET's Redaktion at nedennævnte danske Frivillige er faldet paa Østfronten i Kampen mod Bolchevismen

Viggo Peitersen	f. 2.- 4.-20	Nørre Allé 11, København.
Erik Christiansen	f. 3.- 9.-17	Kildevældsgade 47, København.
Verner Meisner	f. 13.-10.-21	Vibekegade 12, København.
Svend Skov	f. 14.-12.-12	Jernbanegade, Grindsted.
Osvald Henry Larsen	f. 6.- 2.-11	Tilmeldt i Lybæk, ingen Adresse.
Svend Ingermann Jensen	f. 13.-10.-21	Herrestrup, Grevinge, Holbæk Amt.
Gerhard Bentsen	f. 18.- 2.-19	Taasingegade 45 St. tv., København.
Karl Holger Nielsen	f. 31.- 3.-15	Tebbestrupvej 27, Randers.
Ejner Markersen	f. 17.- 3.-12	Kildebæksvej 28, Svendborg.
Svend-Erik Nielsen	f. 5.-11.-19	Nordtoften 13, København.
Harry Andersen	f. 29.- 6.-16	Haveforeningen D.S.B., Gl. Køgevej.
Ole Jorgensen	f. 31.- 7.-22	Taarnborg, Korsør.
Borge Nyrup Larsen	f. 22.- 7.-22	Femø pr. Bandholm.
Otto Schmidt	f. 3.- 1.-17	Østergade 83, Esbjerg.

Ære være deres Minde

The Danish newspaper *Faedrelandet* often listed the fallen.

Death notices for *Freikorps Danmark* soldiers from Danish newspaper *Faedrelandet*.

Partimdl., SS-Frivillig, Sturmmann

Aksel Blomme

af Thorohuse pr. Assens, er faldet paa Østfronten i Kampen mod Kommunismen.

For Danmarks Ære, Frihed og Ret.

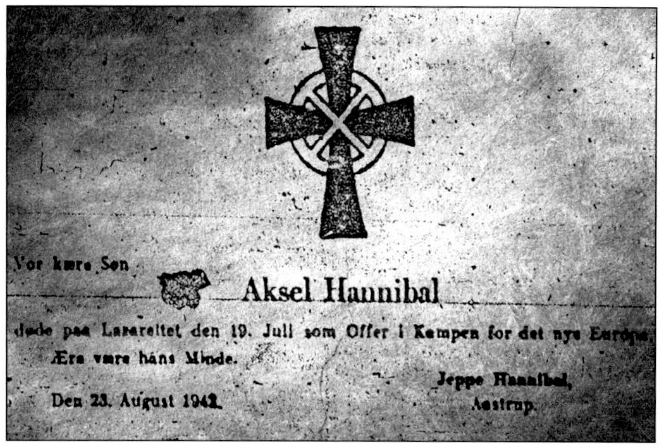

Vor kære Søn

Aksel Hannibal

døde paa Lazarettet den 19. Juli som Offer i Kampen for det nye Europa.

Ære være hans Minde.

Jeppe Hannibal,
Aastrup.

Den 23. August 1942.

Vor kære Søn og Broder

Oberscharführer Alfred Thyssen Oksen

er faldet paa Østfronten den 22. Maj 1942.

Paa Familiens Vegne.

Alfred Oksen, Højvang

Mindegudstjeneste afholdes den 10. August Kl. 15.00 i Vodder Kirke.
Deltagerne bedes derefter samles i Frifelt Kro.

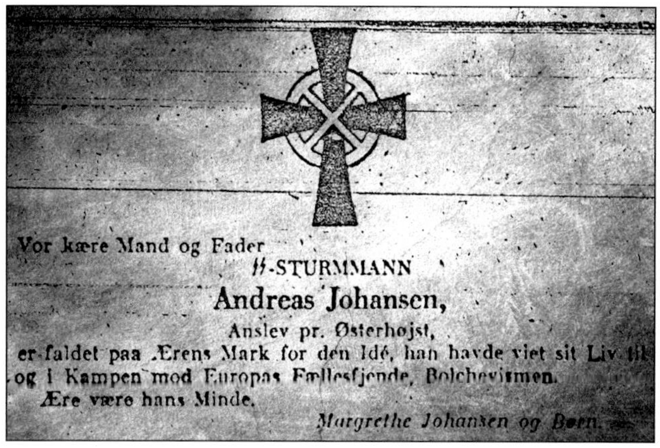

Vor kære Mand og Fader

SS-STURMMANN

Andreas Johansen,

Anslev pr. Østerhøjst,

er faldet paa Ærens Mark for den Idé, han havde viet sit Liv til og i Kampen mod Europas Fællesfjende, Bolchevismen.

Ære være hans Minde.

Margrethe Johansen og Børn.

Det meddeles herved at min kære Mand, mine Børns gode Fader, Oberschütze i Frikorps »Danmark«

Børge Jensen

er død den 23. Maj. Æret være hans Minde.

Riis Skov d. 15. Juli 1942.

Bodil Jensen og Børnene,
M. Mejersvej 13.

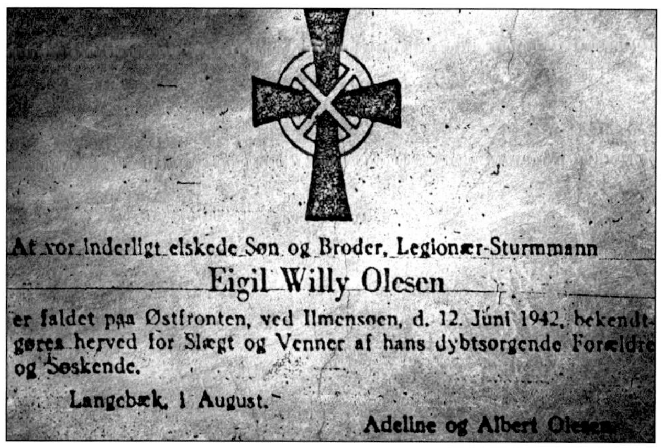

At vor inderligt elskede Søn og Broder, Legionær-Sturmmann

Eigil Willy Olesen

er faldet paa Østfronten, ved Ilmensøen, d. 12. Juni 1942, bekendtgøres herved for Slægt og Venner af hans dybtsørgende Forældre og Søskende.

Langebæk, 1 August.

Adeline og Albert Olesen.

Vor kære, trofaste Kammerat

Ejnar Hansen

er faldet paa Ærens Mark i Kampen mod Bolchevismen d. 30. Juli 1942, 22 Aar gammel.

Ære være hans Minde!

Give Afdeling.

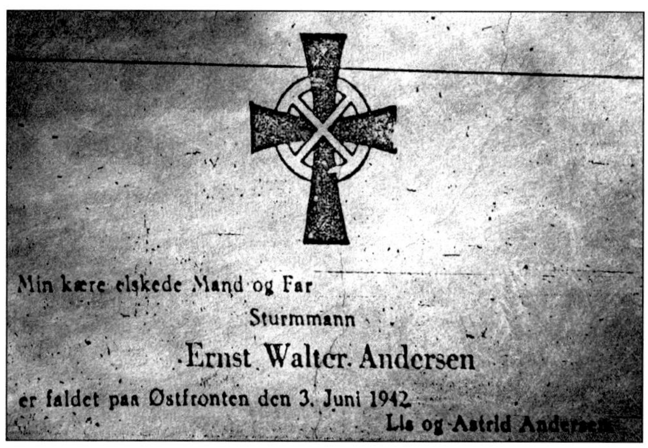

Min kære elskede Mand og Far

Sturmmann

Ernst Walter Andersen

er faldet paa Østfronten den 3. Juni 1942.

Lis og Astrid Andersen.

Vor gode Kammerater

Frivillig i Frikorps »Danmark«

Ejner Markersen

† 2. Juni 1942.

Frivillig i Frikorps »Danmark«

Poul G. Andersen

† 11. Juni 1942.

Faldne i ærefuld Kamp paa Europas Østfront.

Ære være jeres Minde.

DNSAP, Svendborg Afdeling.

Vor kære Søn og Broder, Storhirdfører i N.S.U.

Erik Jensen

er den 29. Maj 1942 død for en Idé, der var ham hellig.

Helene og Oscar Jensen, Povl, Gerda, Manne.

Vore kære Søn, Broder og Svoger

Sturmmann Erik Trojan

Indehaver af Jernkorset af 2. Klasse,

er faldet paa Ærens Mark i Kampen mod Bolchevismen den 11. Juni 1942.

Familien TROJAN, Gråsten.

Vor kære eneste Søn og Broder

Frede Nikolaj Damgaard Andersen

er falden paa Østfronten.

I dyb Sorg Familien

Jakob Andersen, Gl. Sognefogedgaard, Ejstrupholm.

Mindegudstjenste afholdes Lørdag d. 1. August Kl. 14 i Ejstrupholm Kirke.

I urokkelig Tro paa Fører og Idé er vor kære Mand og Søn

Løjtnant, Untersturmführer

Hans Carl Nordholm

faldet paa Østfronten den 24. Maj 1942 i heltemodig Kamp mod Verdensfjenden. — Ære være hans Minde.

DE EFTERLADTE.

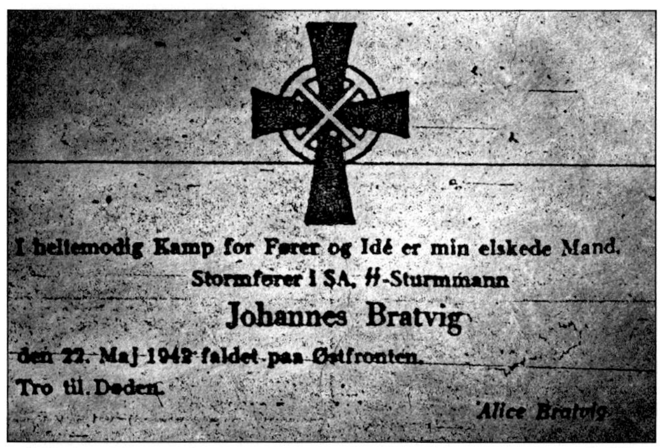

I heltemodig Kamp for Fører og Idé er min elskede Mand,

Stormfører i SA, ᛋᛋ-Sturmmann

Johannes Bratvig

den 22. Maj 1942 faldet paa Østfronten.

Tro til Døden.

Alice Bratvig.

Vor kære Nevø og Fætter

Løjtnant Johannes Just Nielsen

Untersturmführer i Frikorps »Danmark«,

er faldet ved Østfronten den 28. Maj i heltemodig Kamp mod Bolchevismen, 22 Aar gammel.

EBBA JØRGENSEN. CHR. JØRGENSEN, Afdelingsingeniør.
VAGN JØRGENSEN. STEN JØRGENSEN.

Min kære Dreng, min eneste Søn,

Karl Holger Nielsen

ᛋᛋ-Rottenführer, S.A.-Gruppefører

kæmpede og faldt for Danmarks Ære mod Bolchevismen 2. Juni 1942.

Paa hele Familiens Vegne:
N. E. Nielsen og Hustru, Vesterport 6, Randers.

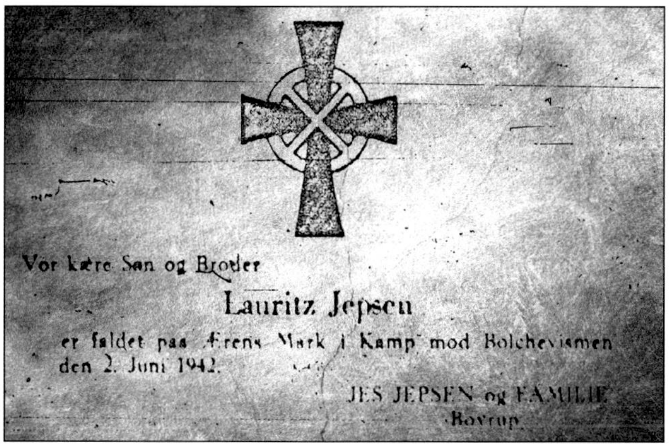
Vor kære Søn og Broder
Lauritz Jepsen
er faldet paa Ærens Mark i Kamp mod Bolchevismen
den 2. Juni 1942.
JES JEPSEN og FAMILIE
Bovrup

Vor kære Søn og Broder
Christen Madsen Brødersen
Premierløjtnant, ϟϟ-Obersturmführer,
er som dansk Frivillig faldet paa Østfronten den 17. Juni for en
Idé, der var ham hellig.
FAMILIEN BRODERSEN
»Egeskov«, Ullerup

Vor kære Søn og Broder
Martin Peter Sundboll Feddersen
er falden paa Østfronten den 11. Juni.
Hvil i Fred, kære Dreng. I dyb Sorg
Familien Feddersen, Bollemose,

Vor gode Kammerat, Rottenführer
Niels Chr. Jensen
er faldet paa Østfronten den 25. Maj 1942.
Paa 4. Distrikts Vegne.
HANS JOHANNSEN
Mindeappel den 12. August Kl. 20, Frederikssundsvej
(Brønshøj Selskabslokaler).

Min elskede Mand
Fylkefører, Unterscharführer
Oscar Birkmar
er faldet paa Østfronten d. 11. Juni.
Skal vi end ofre Livet, falder vi for vort Land.
Inger Birkmar

Vore kære lille Broder og Svoger
ϟϟ-SCHÜTZE
PAUL DÜSTERDICH
er faldet paa Østfronten, knapt 20 Aar gammel, i Kampen for det
nye Europa.
Ære være hans Minde.
København, den 29. August 1942.
Børge og Alice Parbst
f. Düsterdich

Vore kære og eneste Søn
Preben Jensen
er som dansk Frivillig faldet paa Østfronten den 2. Juni for en
Idé, der var ham hellig.
ELLA og L. MAR. JENSEN,
Kerteminde.

Min elskede Mand, vore Børns altopofrende Fader
Unterscharführer
Sigfred Bjergbæk
er falden i Rusland den 6. Juni 1942 for en Idé, der var ham hellig.
I dyb Sorg
Johanne Bjergbæk og

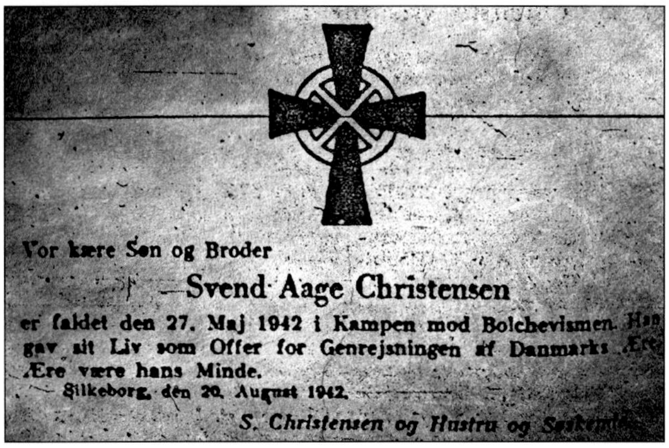
Vor kære Søn og Broder
Svend Aage Christensen
er faldet den 27. Maj 1942 i Kampen mod Bolchevismen.
gav sit Liv som Offer for Genrejsningen af Danmarks
Ære være hans Minde.
Silkeborg, den 20. August 1942.
S. Christensen og Hustru og

Min elskede Søn, vor kære Broder, Kontorist
Gerhard Viggo Damgaard Bentzen
er den 2. Juni faldet paa Østfronten i Kampen mod Kommunismen
Ved Ofre skabtes Danmarks Ære!
Gunnar, Georg, Bent, Henny, Christian Bentzen,
Taasingegade 45.

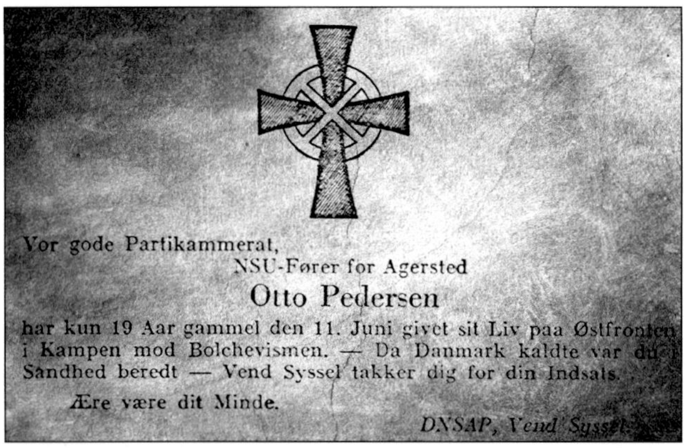
Vor gode Partikammerat,
NSU-Fører for Agersted
Otto Pedersen
har kun 19 Aar gammel den 11. Juni givet sit Liv paa Østfronten
i Kampen mod Bolchevismen. — Da Danmark kaldte var du
Sandhed beredt — Vend Syssel takker dig for din Indsats.
Ære være dit Minde.
DNSAP, Vend Syssel.

Vor trofaste Kammerat
Peder Mørch Pedersen
er faldet paa Østfronten i Kampen mod Kommunismen
Ved Ofre skabtes Danmarks Ære.
S.A.-Kammerater i Stenum

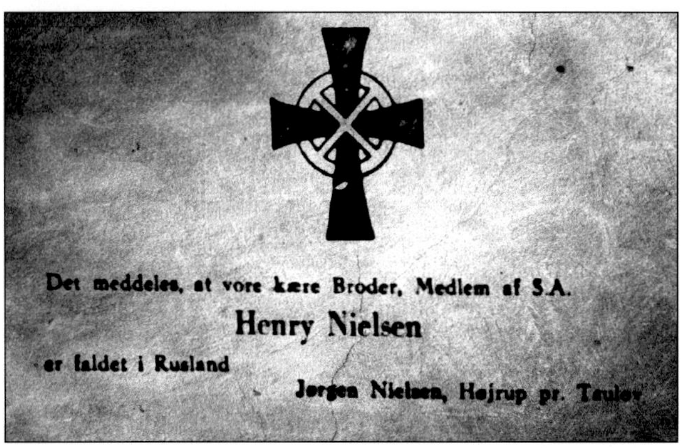
Det meddeles, at vore kære Broder, Medlem af S.A.
Henry Nielsen
er faldet i Rusland
Jørgen Nielsen, Højrup pr.

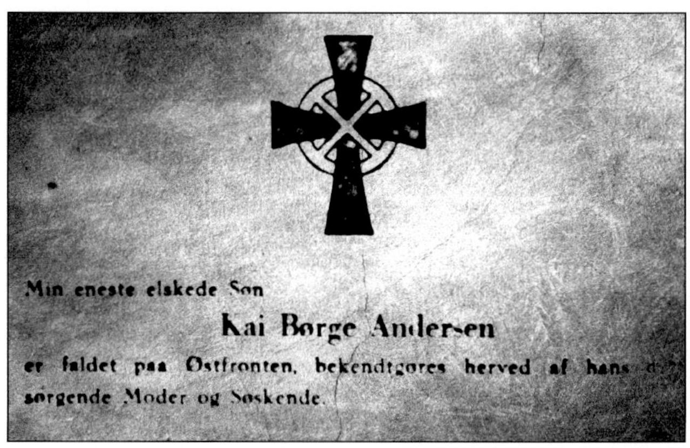
Min eneste elskede Søn
Kai Børge Andersen
er faldet paa Østfronten, bekendtgøres herved af hans
sørgende Moder og Søskende.

kære Søn og Broder
SS-STURMMANN
Peter Bernhard Petersen
er faldet paa Østfronten den 20. Juli 1942 i Kampen for den
Sag, som var ham hellig.
Hans Forældre og Broder i Odense.

elskede Mand og vore Børns tapre Far
Unterscharführer Aage Dyring
faldet paa Østfronten den 2. Juni.
Æret være hans Minde!
Valborg Dyring og
Bredegade 68,

Det meddeles Slægt og Venner, at min kære Mand, mine Børns altopofrende og kærlige Fader,
Legn. Schütze
Poul Otto Larsen
efter lang Tids Sygdom er afgaaet ved Døden paa et Lazaret i Belgrad den 27. September 1942.
Jenny Larsen.
Anne-Lise, Gull-May, Hanne og lille Per.
Hvil i Fred Kære.

Vor elskede Søn, Forlovede, Broder, Svoger og Onkel
Mads Madsen Christensen
er falden i Rusland den 6. Juni 1942.
I dyb Sorg.
Familien Hans P. Christensen, Honkys.
Hans Forlovede Didde Hansen.
Familien Lausen, Møgeltønder.

Vor Kammerat, Frivillig i Frikorps »Danmark«
Svend Agner Nielsen
† 11. Juni 1942.
Faldt i Kampen for Danmarks Ære.
Du stred den gode Strid.
Fredensborg Afdeling.

Min elskede Mand og Fader, SS Legionær Schütze
Egon Steinlein
er den 19. Juli 1942 faldet paa Østfronten i Kamp for en Idé, som var ham hellig.
Ære være dit Minde!
Elisabeth Steinlein og lille Poul Erik.

Min kære Fætter, vor bedste Ven, SS Legionær Schütze
Jørgen Hardy Jørgensen
haardt saaret i Kampen mod Bolchevismen den 19. Juli 1942, er død den 12. Januar 1943 som Følge af sine Saar paa et Lazaret i Danmark. Æret være hans Minde!
København, den 13. Januar 1943.
Molly, Margrethe og Poul Jensen.

Vor kære eneste Søn, Broder og Svoger
SS-Oberscharführer
AXEL GRAABECH
(Jernkors og Stormabz.)
døde Torsdag den 22. April af sine Saar efter 9 Maaneders Sygeleje paa Krigslazaret i Fredericia, 31 Aar gammel.
Minna og Johannes Graabech,
Tove Graabech,
Ellen og Hans Møller.
NB. Begravelsen har fundet Sted i Esbjerg.

Min tapre Soldaterkammerat, Oberscharführer O. W. Jensen fandt i tapreste Indsats Heltedøden for Danmarks Ære under Kamp mod Bolchevikerne den 17. Maj 1942.
Hans Navn vil leve evigt, og vi sørger for, at hans Daad ikke bliver forgæves.
(sign.)
v. Schalburg
SS Sturmbannführer og
Chef for Frikorps „Danmark“.

4

Freikorps Danmark on leave of absence in Denmark 8 September-13 October 1942

On 4 August 1942, when *Freikorps Danmark* was withdrawn from the Demyansk Pocket, it was a decimated and worn-out unit. After three months of intense battle, some of the soldiers were suffering from swamp fever (malaria) and many other skin diseases. They had been in a battle which was fought not just against the Russians, but also against the poor conditions at the front in the Pocket. The only bright side was that the soldiers at last had a long leave of absence back home in Denmark.

Grand tribute?

Freikorps Danmark expected that they would come back home and be praised for their effort for the 'homeland'. The DNSAP, the Danish Nazi party with Fritz Clausen at its head, had huge expectations. The DNSAP hoped that the arrival of the volunteers in Copenhagen would create a grand triumphal procession, which could be used for propaganda to enlist more volunteers. *Freikorps Danmark* hoped for a grand tribute from the people as they marched through the Danish capital. However, things turned out very differently. The general attitude of the Danish population had changed since the establishment of *Freikorps Danmark*. Although the Danish government still collaborated with the Germans, the attitude among the civilians was completely different. On 8 September, the special train from Germany arrived at Copenhagen's *Godsbanegaarden* (goods depot), containing approximately 850 of the volunteer soldiers. Since *Freikorps Danmark*'s withdrawal from the front in the Demyansk Pocket, they had been in isolation at Mitau in Latvia due to a breakout of typhus fever. At the goods depot, many relatives, *NSU* (national socialist youth) boys and girls as well as DNSAP sympathisers, were there to meet the returning *Freikorps Danmark*. K.B. Martinsen, the commander of the *Freikorps*, made a brief speech there for those who were assembled. Thereafter, the soldiers marched to '*Kastellet*' (The Citadel). From there, the four companies were sent to their quarters: two of the companies were quartered at Baadsmands-straedes barracks and the other two at Artillerivejens barracks. The march through the streets of Copenhagen was a bad experience for them. They were met by a population who had no sympathy for them, with the *Freikorps Danmark* volunteers met by shouting and abusive language. They had certainly not expected this kind of welcome. The volunteers stayed in Copenhagen until 11 September, after which about half of them travelled back to their families around the country. Before they left Copenhagen, they participated in a propaganda march through the city, and later finished off with a night among comrades in '*K.B. Hallen*' (The Hall of K.B.). The rest of the leave was marred by a number of difficult episodes, and many volunteers reported harassment, provocation etc. to the police. One of the worst examples happened when trouble led to a fight at Christianshavn between soldiers of *Freikorps Danmark* and workers of the B & W shipyard. In general, the period of leave was marked by trouble everywhere, but it was worst in the major cities.

Back to the front

On 13 October, when the leave of *Freikorps Danmark* ended, it proved to be the first and last time the volunteers had a joint period of leave. The reason was the amount of trouble it aroused; subsequently, the volunteers were sent on leave of absences in small groups. On 13 October, *Freikorps Danmark* reported to Artillerivejens barracks. A grand farewell parade was held, where the commander-in-chief of the combined German forces in Denmark, General Hermann von Hanneken, and *Brigadeführer* Paul Ernst Kanstein were present. Also in attendance was Danish general Ebbe Goertz, who inspected the volunteer corps. Shortly thereafter, a special train departed for Latvia, where *Freikorps Danmark* trained and made ready for winter war in Velikije Luki, Russia.

Freikorps Danmark's tramp of boots in Copenhagen in 1942. (Photo: Private)

Godsbanegaarden in Copenhagen. *Freikorps Danmark* arriving on their leave. (Photo: Rigborg Dahl Nielsen)

Crowds gather for *Freikorps Danmark*'s arrival on their leave of absence. (Photo: Rigborg Dahl Nielsen)

Freikorps Danmark in front of the *Godsbanegaarden* in Copenhagen. (Photo: Private)

Soldiers of *Freikorps Danmark* received flowers from those who attended. (Photo: Private)

A soldier of *Freikorps Danmark* who received flowers and a flag. (Photo: Private)

Frits Clausen of the DNSAP (Danish Nazi Party) made a speech for *Freikorps Danmark*. (Photo: Private)

K.B. Martinsen, Commander of *Freikorps Danmark*, in front of the *Godsbanegaarden*. (Photo: Private)

The soldiers of *Freikorps Danmark* lined up in front of the *Godsbanegaarden*. (Photo: Rigborg Dahl Nielsen)

The Commander, K.B. Martinsen, made a speech about the deeds of *Freikorps Danmark* in the Demyansk Pocket on the Eastern Front in the summer of 1942. (Photo: Private)

A photograph taken from the top of the train showing the start of the march to Copenhagen city centre. (Photo: Rigborg Dahl Nielsen)

There were many flowers from those who turned out to greet the volunteer Danish soldiers. (Photo: Private)

The march to Copenhagen city centre begins. (Photo: Rigborg Dahl Nielsen)

Company commander Per Soerensen leading *Freikorps Danmark* in the march. (Photo: Private)

Many turned out to watch *Freikorps Danmark* march through the streets of Copenhagen. (Photo: National Museum)

Enthusiastic crowds greeted those marching through the streets of Copenhagen. (Photo: Private)

Company commander Per Soerensen leading *Freikorps Danmark* through Copenhagen. (Photo: Private)

Flowers were strewn in the streets for *Freikorps Danmark*'s march through Copenhagen. (Photo: Private)

Freikorps Danmark and their supporters marching through the streets of Copenhagen. (Photo: Rigborg Dahl Nielsen)

Many supporters followed the march through Copenhagen. (Photo: National Museum)

Mounted police were also present during the march. (Photo: National Museum)

A company of the volunteer soldiers of *Freikorps Danmark* march through the crowds. (Photo: Rigborg Dahl Nielsen)

The heavy tramp of Nazi boots through the streets of Copenhagen. (Photo: Private)

A German orchestra formed part of the march through the streets of Copenhagen. (Photo: Private)

K.B. Martinsen riding a horse during the march. One of the crowd shouted: "That sure is an odd horse, its asshole is on its back!" It is said that Martinsen took the insult with a smile. (Photo: Private)

The girls liked the handsome soldiers of *Freikorps Danmark*. (Photo: Private)

Some of the crowd were arrested during the march by the police and *Waffen-SS*. (Photo: Private)

Soldiers of *Freikorps Danmark* drinking after the march. (Photo: Private)

Soldiers of *Freikorps Danmark* eating after the march in Copenhagen. (Photo: Private)

Their leave ended on 13 October 1942, when *Freikorps Danmark* assembled again. (Photo: Private)

Freikorps Danmark assembled in Copenhagen when the leave of absence ended on 13 October 1942. (Photo: Private)

Copenhagen train station: *Freikorps Danmark* soldiers returning to the front. (Photo: Private)

5

Velikije Luki in Russia 5 December 1942-24 March 1943

After the leave of absence of *Freikorps Danmark*, they travelled from Copenhagen to Mitau in Latvia. *Freikorps Danmark* stayed there until the middle of November 1942, when it was transferred to the town of Bobruisk in the current Belarus. In Mitau, *Freikorps Danmark* received practical training for winter war. The idea was that the unit should be deployed to combat partisans in Belarus. The Danish volunteers were assigned to 1st *SS*-Brigade, which was infamous for its brutal combat against partisans. On 19 November, when major Russian forces attacked, everything changed. After this, *Freikorps Danmark* was sent to the front instead of fighting partisans. The Russians attacked around the town of Velikije Luki, hoping to drive a wedge between the German Army Group North and Army Group South. The purpose of the attack was to cut off the whole of the middle and northern part of the German front and press them against the Baltic. The Germans faced a grave situation, as a Russian breakthrough would cause the Germans to lose control of this section of the front. During the attack, the Russians trapped about 7,500 Germans soldiers in Velikije Luki. On 5 December, *Freikorps Danmark* arrived with a force of approximately 1,100 soldiers at the town of Nevel, south-west of Velikije Luki. After a couple of days, the various companies were brought to the frontline. The corps had to defend part of a very thinly fortified frontline at the railroads between Velikije Luki and Nevel. The companies of *Freikorps Danmark* were deployed north of the town of Bobrikowo, where they had to cover an area of 5km. This meant that each company held about 1.5km. Their positions consisted of small bunkers, which were connected by paths through the huge masses of snow. On several occasions, however, the Russians managed to get through the relatively thinly held or undefended German lines. The Danes continually sent out patrols to the undefended lines, which resulted in minor clashes with the Russians, with several killed and wounded. Unlike the summer effort in the Demyansk Pocket, snow and temperatures down to minus 30 degrees marked the battlefield. As the cold got worse, more cold-related injuries were reported. Lice, skin rashes and having to stay in the cold bunkers were major problems for the *Freikorps* soldiers. On 19 December, *Freikorps Danmark* shifted its position to the west, to the towns of Laskaturino, Kondratowo and Taidy. Since the corps had redeployed to the front, they had experienced only a few brief battles against the Russian forces. However, the Danes were to participate in two major battles against the Russians. The first was on Christmas Eve in 1942, which is elaborated in Chapter 9.

The second major battle – at the town of Taidy

After the battles of Christmas 1942, that part of the front was relatively quiet. The small town of Taidy, which the Russians had occupied for a while, was a major nuisance for the Germans. It was therefore decided that a major attack should be launched at the town in February 1943. Taidy was in a lofty location, from where the Russians had a good view of the area, including the railroad between Velikije Luki and Nevel. The town had been rebuilt by the Russians as a veritable fortress, containing many underground passages, tunnels and observation posts for their artillery. Commanded by *Obersturmführer* Heinz Henneke, the Germans attacked and defeated the Russians in their positions, after which the Pioneer Platoon of *Freikorps Danmark* blew up the fortress. Their remaining time at the front, until 20 March 1943, was relatively quiet. From that date, the corps started withdrawing its soldiers from the frontline area, and four days later its position was taken by the 1st *SS*-Brigade. After this, *Freikorps Danmark* was sent by train to Grafenwöhr barracks in southern Germany. Total losses for *Freikorps Danmark* in the winter fighting around Velikije Luki in 1942-43 was 44 soldiers and an unknown number of wounded.

(See page 393 of the appendix for a supplementary text to this chapter.)

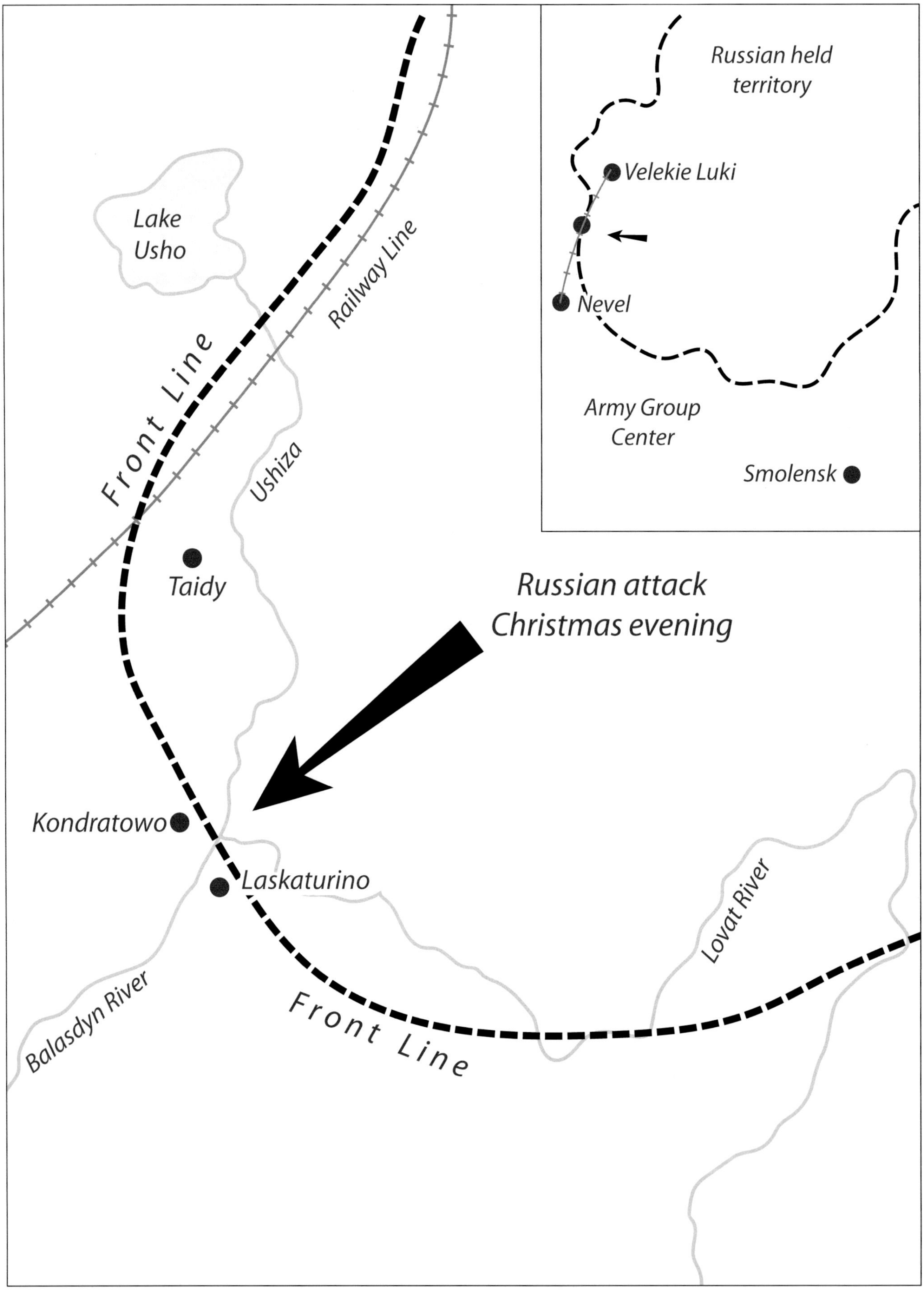

Freikorps Danmark's positions at the front in 1942-43 at the railroad between Velikije Luki and Nevel in Russia. (Map by George Anderson based on sketch by Lasse Larsen)

Soldiers of *Freikorps Danmark* in winter gear with supplies in front of a bunker. (Photo: Private)

Fritz Adler, a soldier of *Freikorps Danmark*, outside his bunker. (Photo: Private)

Soldiers of *Freikorps Danmark* in a command bunker. (Photo: Private)

An unknown soldier in a trench outside a bunker. (Photo: Private)

Unknown soldiers of *Freikorps Danmark* smoking pipes outside a Russian cottage. (Photo: Private)

Commander K.B. Martinsen (left) with Eduard Hein, a German. (Photo: Private)

Magnus Moeller, a motorcycle dispatch rider for the *Freikorps*. (Photo: Magnus Moeller)

An unknown motorcycle dispatch rider of *Freikorps Danmark*. (Photo: Jann Hornum)

Unterscharführer Knud Per Dahl Nielsen in the Russian winter. (Photo: Rigborg Dahl Nielsen)

Soldiers of *Freikorps Danmark* receive honours following the battles against the Russians. (Photo: Private)

An unknown soldier of *Freikorps Danmark*. (Photo: Rigborg Dahl Nielsen)

Two unknown soldiers of *Freikorps Danmark*. (Photo: Private)

Soldiers of *Freikorps Danmark* photographed outside the house where they were stationed. (Photo: Jann Hornum)

A group of unknown soldiers of *Freikorps Danmark* in front of a bunker. (Photo: Private)

Vehicles fighting through a muddy Russian road. (Photo: Jann Hornum)

A house where soldiers of *Freikorps Danmark* were probably quartered. (Photo: Private)

An unknown soldier of *Freikorps Danmark* with a truck. (Photo: Jann Hornum)

Soldiers of *Freikorps Danmark* with some Russian children. (Photo: Private)

Nude bathing in the snow next to the railroad. (Photo: Private)

Soldiers relieve themselves by the railroad. (Photo: Poul Christensen)

Freddy Boerge Vilhelm Hansen outside his bunker. (Photo: Poul Christensen)

Two unknown soldiers of *Freikorps Danmark* in winter clothing. (Photo: Poul Christensen)

The *Dannebrog* flutters in the wind on the roof, while a group of soldiers of *Freikorps Danmark* pose for the photographer. (Photo: Private)

An unknown soldier of *Freikorps Danmark* poses for the photographer. (Photo: Jann Hornum)

Martin Ingemann Bruun Olesen, a soldier of *Freikorps Danmark*, relaxes with his pipe. (Photo: Jann Hornum)

Per Soerensen (left), commander of the 1st Company, with an unknown soldier. (Photo: Jann Hornum)

Unknown soldiers of *Freikorps Danmark* smoking cigarettes. (Photo: Rigborg Dahl Nielsen)

A relaxed group of unknown soldiers of *Freikorps Danmark*. (Photo: Rigborg Dahl Nielsen)

Unknown soldiers of *Freikorps Danmark* fooling around in front of the camera. (Photo: Rigborg Dahl Nielsen)

An unknown *Hauptscharführer* of *Freikorps Danmark*. (Photo: Rigborg Dahl Nielsen)

Unknown soldiers of *Freikorps Danmark* share a joke. (Photo: Rigborg Dahl Nielsen)

An unknown soldier of *Freikorps Danmark* poses for the camera. (Photo: Rigborg Dahl Nielsen)

Unknown soldiers of *Freikorps Danmark* on duty next to the railway line. (Photo: Rigborg Dahl Nielsen)

Unknown soldiers of *Freikorps Danmark* relax outside their cabin. (Photo: Rigborg Dahl Nielsen)

A machine gun mounted inside a German bunker. (Photo: Rigborg Dahl Nielsen)

Unknown soldiers of *Freikorps Danmark* with a motorcycle and sidecar. (Photo: Rigborg Dahl Nielsen)

Per Soerensen, commander of the 1st Company. (Photo: Rigborg Dahl Nielsen)

Per Soerensen (right), commander of the 1st Company, talks with other officers. (Photo: Rigborg Dahl Nielsen)

Unknown soldiers of *Freikorps Danmark* enjoy a meal and a cigarette. (Photo: Rigborg Dahl Nielsen)

The view from a bunker over a wintry landscape. (Photo: Rigborg Dahl Nielsen)

Unknown soldiers of *Freikorps Danmark* joke with a young Russian woman. (Photo: Rigborg Dahl Nielsen)

Unterscharführer Knud Per Dahl Nielsen. He later died in the Battle of Narva in Estonia on 13 February 1944. (Photo: Rigborg Dahl Nielsen)

Freikorps Danmark travelled by freight train to southern Germany. (Photo: Rigborg Dahl Nielsen)

Freikorps Danmark soldiers prepare to leave by train for southern Germany. (Photo: Private)

Freikorps Danmark soldiers travelled with their vehicles by freight train to southern Germany. (Photo: Private)

Vehicles and men are made ready for the rail journey to southern Germany. (Photo: Private)

Poul Neergaard Jacobsen (centre) with two unknown comrades. (Photo: Rigborg Dahl Nielsen)

A total of 44 soldiers of *Freikorps Danmark* had been killed in the fighting, among them N. Andresen. (Photo: Private)

Ny Hæder til Frikorps „Danmark"s Soldater

En Række Ordensdekorationer efter heltemodig Indsats paa Østfronten

Kort Tid efter at Frikorps »Danmark« havde forladt Danmark efter en velfortjent Orlov, gik Korpset paany til Indsats paa Østfronten. Under Kampene her har de Frivillige atter vist, hvilke gode Soldateregenskaber de er i Besiddelse af, paa alle Maader har de vist Heltemod og Opofrelse, og dette er nu for en Række Frivilliges Vedkommende resulteret i en Række Udnævnelser. De dekorerede er følgende:

E. K. I:	Leg. - Ustuf. Poulsen, Eigil	11. 1. 43
E. K. II:	ᛋᛋ-Ostuf. Worsöe Larsen, Bent	24. 12. 42
	ᛋᛋ-Oscha. Adler, Fritz	24. 12. 42
	Leg.-Uscha. Jørgensen, Jørgen	24. 12. 42
	ᛋᛋ-Uscha. Schadt, Jacob	24. 12. 42
	Leg.-Oscha. Nielsen, Jens	24. 12. 42
	Leg.-Strm. Jensen, S. Kaj Svinning	11. 1. 43
	Leg. Strm. Petersen, Tage Møller	11. 1. 43
	Leg.-Strm. Friis, Olaf S. Jacob	11. 1. 43

Bisher verliehene KVK.s (Kriegsverdienstkreuze):

K.V.K. II:	Leg.-Uscha. Skovmøller, Axel	21. 10. 42
	Leg.-Uscha. Jensen, Broder	21. 10. 42
	Leg.-Uscha. Czech, Bernhard	21. 12. 42
	Leg.-Uscha. Thomsen, Verner Kühn	21. 10. 42
	Leg.-Uscha. Olesen, Kai	21. 12. 42
	Leg.-Rottf. Petersen, Werner	21. 10. 42

Danes who received the German Iron Cross.

Death notices from Danish newspaper *Faedrelandet*.

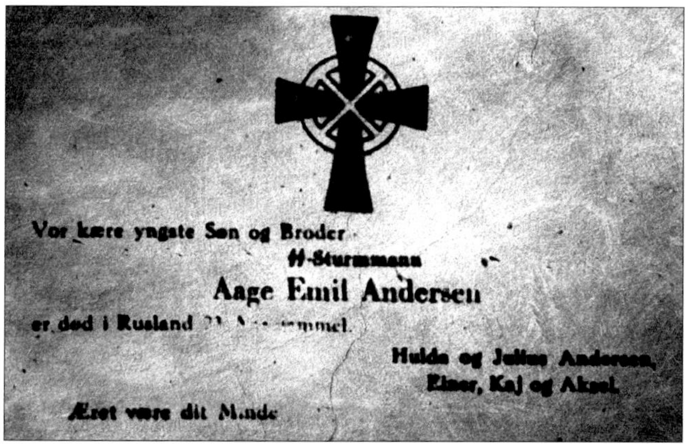

ᛋᛋ Rottenführer
Carl Martin Rasmussen
Æret være dit Navn!

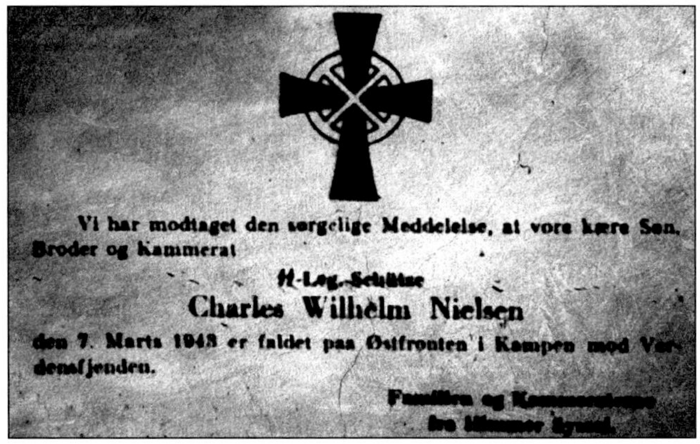
Vi har modtaget den sørgelige Meddelelse, at vore kære Søn, Broder og Kammerat
Charles Wilhelm Nielsen
den 7. Marts 1943 er faldet paa Østfronten i Kampen mod Verdensfjenden.

ᛋᛋ SCHÜTZE
Frede Ib Emil Schlichter
Æret være hans Minde

Unterscharführer
GUNNAR DANIELSEN
Ved Ofre skabtes Danmarks Ære!

Vor kære Søn og Broder
ᛋᛋ STURMMANN
Hans Peter Frederiksen
er faldet paa Østfronten den 3. December 1942 i Kampen mod Kommunismen. — Han døde for at vi andre kan leve.
Æret være hans Minde

H. P. K. Andersen
Æret være hans Minde
København, Februar 1943

Vor gode Ven og Kammerat
Jens Carl Martin Johannsen,
Æret være hans Minde.

Min elskede Mand, Legionærskytte i »Frikorps Danmark«
Jens Peder Precht
er faldet i Kampen paa Østfronten mod Verdensfjenden den 23. Januar 1943. Æret være hans Minde!

Det bekendtgøres herved, at min kære Forlovede og bedste Kammerat — vor gode Svigersøn

ϟϟ-Rottenführer

KAJ ENNA

har fundet Heltedøden paa Østfronten den 27. Februar 1943.

Ved Ofre skabtes Danmarks Ære.

Jytte Kjeldorg
V. Kjeldorg og Hustru

Jeg har modtaget den sørgelige Meddelelse, at min eneste Søn,
ϟϟ-Leg. Rottenführer

Kaj Aage Jensen

Natten mellem 2. og 3. Marts 1943 er faldet paa Østfronten, 17 Aar gammel.

Enkefru Gundine Jensen, Kongensgade 12, Odense.

Karl August Nellemann

Vor gode Kammerat
ϟϟ ROTTENFÜHRER

Nicolaj Johs. Andresen

Indehaver af E. K. II
er faldet paa Ukens Mark i Kamp mod Verdensfjenden
Ære være hans Minde

Poul Ejnar Hansen

Lis Hansen Lille Hanne Forældre og Søskende
Vær beredt for Danmark
Ved Ofre skabtes Danmarks Ære

Vor kære Søn og Broder,

SA 11 a20 — ϟϟ Rottenführer

Hans Henrik Langgaard-Nielsen

er tro mod Fører og Fædreland faldet paa Østfronten den 25. Februar 1943 i heltemodig Kamp mod Bolchevismen

København, den 13. Marts 1943.

Ved Ofre skabes Danmarks Ære

Anna og A. Langgaard-Nielsen
Elmer Langgaard-Nielsen (p. t. RAD, Hjerlshagen).

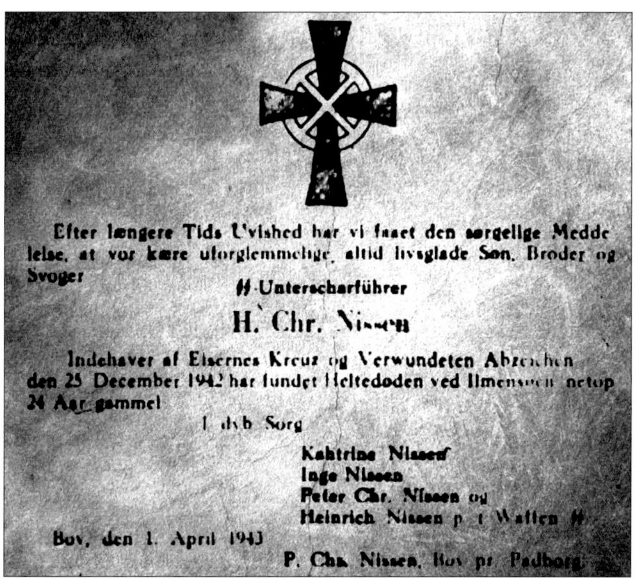

Efter længere Tids Uvished har vi faaet den sørgelige Meddelelse, at vor kære uforglemmelige, altid livsglade Søn, Broder og Svoger

ϟϟ-Unterscharführer

H. Chr. Nissen

Indehaver af Eisernes Kreuz og Verwundeten Abzeichen den 25. December 1942 har fundet Heltedøden ved Ilmensøen netop 24 Aar gammel.

I dyb Sorg

Kathrine Nissen
Inge Nissen
Peter Chr. Nissen og
Heinrich Nissen p. t. Waffen ϟϟ

Bov, den 1. April 1943

P. Chr. Nissen, Bov pr. Padborg.

6

The abolition of *Freikorps Danmark*, Grafenwöhr, 20 May 1943

On 24 March 1943, *Freikorps Danmark* withdrew from the battles at Velikije Luki/Nevel, and approximately 900 of its men were sent by train to Grafenwöhr barracks in Germany. Grafenwöhr was a major barracks, with a capacity for 60,000 soldiers. At the beginning of May 1943, another 250 Danish volunteers arrived from the Replacement Company in Bobruisk and Graz in Austria. Since January 1943, rumors had spread that the German high command would abolish the minor independent *SS* units, *Freikorps Danmark* among them.

The abolition of *Freikorps Danmark*

At the start of February 1943, it was at last decided that the small independent *SS* units should dissolve and then be gathered in a division, the *Division Nordland*. The reasons for this included growing unrest among the soldiers, problems in the rear area of the minor *SS* units as well as the units always being assigned to other regiments or divisions. By establishing a new large *SS* division, the Germans hoped to create a new and strong division, and on 6 May, *Regiment 24 Denmark*, the Danish sub-unit of *Division Nordland*, was officially established. At a grand military parade on 20 May, at the barracks in Grafenwöhr, *Freikorps Danmark* was officially abolished. The new commander-in-chief of *Division Nordland* was *Obergruppenführer* Felix Steiner, a German. He participated in the parade, where Danish *SS* volunteers were lined up.

Unrest begins

When it was abolished, *Freikorps Danmark* ceased to be a unit only for Danes, subject to the German *Waffen-SS*. This created mistrust among many of the Danish volunteers, who felt betrayed. This led to a large number of the soldiers of the *Freikorps* wanting to cancel their contract. It did not improve the situation that a large group of Romanians (*Folketyskere*), were now a part of *Regiment 24 Denmark*. This mistrust grew when the head of *Regiment 24 Denmark* was not a Dane neither, but instead a German, *Obersturmbannführer* Hermegild Graf Von Westphalen.

Envoy Mohr arrives

The Germans therefore requested the Danish government send a representative to try to solve the conflict with the Danish *SS* volunteers. On 27 July, envoy Otto Carl Mohr from the barracks in Berlin arrived at Grafenwöhr, where he tried to persuade the volunteers to continue in the *Waffen-SS*. The staff of *Division Nordland*, among them General Felix Steiner, hosted a grand dinner at the castle in Plassenburg, which Otto Carl Mohr attended. On the following day, he visited the Danish volunteers at the barracks in Grafenwöhr, where he, among other things, made a speech to get them to continue to fight, even though *Freikorps Danmark* had already been abolished.

In his speech to the volunteers, he said: "You have joined the battle against our common enemy, Communism, you have already fought bravely alongside our ally, Germany, and you are benefitting our old homeland by continuing the battle until the final victory."

Many of the volunteers saw this speech as a sign of the continued support by officials in Denmark of the volunteers' participation in the war on the German side. However, 300 of the Danish soldiers decided to be relieved of the contracts which they had made with *Waffen-SS*, even though it was difficult for them to do so.

To the front

In late August 1943, *Regiment 24 Denmark* was sent to Croatia along with the rest of *Division Nordland*. There, they were to undergo further training and protect the population against partisan attacks. They were also to be prepared for an Allied landing. Later, *Regiment 24 Denmark* fought tough battles on the Eastern Front for the rest of the war. The Danes of *Regiment 24 Denmark* were among some of the very last *Waffen-SS* units fighting in Berlin in May 1945.

What happened subsequently?

Those Danes who wished to continue the war in *Regiment 24 Denmark* participated in some of the toughest and bloodiest battles of the Eastern Front. Later, some of the volunteers returned home to Denmark, after being declared unfit for battle due to serious war injuries. Thereafter, some of them became members of the Schalburg Corps, which was established by the former commander of *Freikorps Danmark*, K.B. Martinsen. The purpose of the corps was to prevent sabotage in Denmark. Many others were admitted to some of the hated and notorious corps, such as Hipo, '*Sommerkorpset*' (The Summer Corps) etc.

Traitors

For those who during the summer in 1943 were relieved of their contract when *Freikorps Danmark* was abolished, the situation was the same as for those who returned home to Denmark due to war injuries, or were handed over from American, English or Russian captivity. They came back to a country and society that despised them for having participated in the war on the side of the Germans. By late 1944, the Council of Freedom/resistance movement had already made a draft of possible trials against the traitors when the war was over.

Retrospective law

On 1 June 1945, a retrospective law was passed, which went all the way back to 9 April 1940. This meant that those who had joined *Freikorps Danmark*, or other German units, were now considered traitors, even though at the time they had the approval of the Danish government. The penalty for serving the Germans was usually two to four years in prison. However, the penalty was far higher for those who had joined Schalburg, Hipo or '*Sommerkorpset*'. Besides prison, the convicted were deprived of their civilian rights for five years. This meant a loss of the right to vote, retirement pension etc. For the individual, the worst thing was most likely being branded a traitor. In 1945, 1946 and 1947, about 3,500 men were convicted by the courts, with 46 sentenced to death, among them the last commander of *Freikorps Danmark*, K.B. Martinsen. However, this was not for being commander of *Freikorps Danmark* or the Schalburg Corps: he was sentenced to death for shooting and killing another member of Schalburg in the basement of the Freemason lodge in Copenhagen in 1944. This man had been having an affair with his wife. None of the 46 who was sentenced to death were executed for their actions on the Eastern Front, but exclusively for crimes they had committed in Denmark, as members of Hipo Corps or some of the other 'terror' corps.

After prison

Almost none of the *SS* volunteers who were sent to prison stayed for the whole of their sentence. By 1947, the country's attitude had already switched, and many of those who had been jailed were released. Besides the 46 who were executed, another 32 received death sentences but were pardoned. Approximately 275 Danish volunteers ended in Russian captivity during the war, and of those about 75 died of diseases, malnourishment and exhaustion. In 1956, the last Danish volunteer was released from Russian captivity. Over time, almost all of the convicted volunteers went quietly back into Danish society. However, many held a lifelong secret about their past as a soldier in the German *Waffen-SS*.

The retrospective law by which they were sentenced

Law number 259 of 1/6/1945 of Supplement to Civil Penal Code regarding treachery and other injuries to the state.

§1 The decisions of this law are to be used on actions made from 9 April 1940 until one year after the law coming into practice. The Civil Penal Code's regular decisions on the relationship between new and older law is not a hindrance for adjudication in terms of the rules of this law. Those actions, which are mentioned in this law, that happened before 29 August 1943 are exempt from penalty, as long as the offender acted in accordance to law, order or instructions given by a legal Danish authority within its jurisdiction. If the action occurred on or after the aforementioned date, the mentioned sentence can be omitted or the penalty reduced or under special mitigating circumstances be dropped. The decisions in the Civil Penal code §84, subsection 4, number 3, will not be used on actions included in this law.

§2 This law will be used on actions performed by persons, who when they performed the action had Danish citizenship or were a resident in the Danish State, without regard to the action taking place inside or outside the Danish State, and in the final case without consideration if it was punishable in accordance with the law at the scene of the crime. This law also applies to Danes, who after 9 April 1940 have acquired German citizenship. A case for violating this law can be made, even though the offender have been sentenced previously as guilty or not guilty for the action in this country or abroad. Former time served will be deducted from the penalty that is sentenced by this law. If they have been penalized previously for an action, which has not been served, the person will be sentenced to a prison penalty.

§3 The following penalties can be used for actions included in this law: Death sentence and prison. Work house, preventive detention or mental hospital cannot be a penalty in accordance with this law. Conditional sentences cannot be used. Death penalty is carried out by shooting in accordance with the royal decree. The death penalty cannot be given to persons who were under 18 years of age when they committed the crime. A prison term spans from 4 years to a life sentence. However, the penalty cannot be lower than double the Civil Penal Code minimum penalty for that action. Under mitigating circumstances, the penalty can be reduced to one year of prison. If a reduction of penalty is just, the penalty can be reduced to imprisonment for 30 days. Release on parole according to §38 cannot happen. A prisoner will, as soon as possible, be placed in a special penal institution. Rules for serving the penalty will be set by royal decree. Juvenile prisons can only be used, if the offender was under 18 years of age when the crime was committed. Civil Penal Code §84, subsection 1, number 2, last period, cannot be used on actions included in this law.

§4 When a person is judged guilty of a crime in accordance with this law, it can be decided at the sentence, that any fortune or income, in part or in full, can be confiscated for the State Treasury. Disposals, when this was aware to both partners, are invalid. However, should a person's partner be unaware, disposals become invalid.

§5 Fortunes, belonging to Hipo, Sommer, the Schalburg Corps, Danish People Protection or similar associations, which has been connected to, or in any other way supported, the German *Wehrmacht*, will be confiscated for the State Treasury. Knowledge about this will be brought before those of §21, 1 ste Pkt., in the law of supplement to law of the courts' care concerning treatment of cases concerning treason and other actions which can harm the country etc., where the courts will decide, if the conditions for confiscation are present.

§6 If a person is found guilty of a crime, that person is found to be unworthy of common trust. The loss of common trust entails the loss of:

1. The right to vote and eligibility in public affairs.
2. Public service and access to gain public duty and business. The loss does not free the person in focus of doing public duty, which does not rest on a condition of trust.
3. The right to serve in the military. By royal decree, conditions about work duty as substitute for interrupted military service can be arranged.
4. The right to work as a doctor, lawyer or any other position, which requires public authorization.
5. The right to work as a priest for any religious community or to educate in any way.

6. The right to be part of the leadership of, or financially interested in, theatre, movie production or running of cinemas.
7. The right to be a director, president, board member or any other leadership position or position of trust in a business company or union.
8. The right to run independent clinics even on the recommendation of a professional person.
9. The right to retirement pension, social benefit or any other support from the public, if the requirement to gain this is that the person is not found guilty in the public disgraceful action or similar. The right to this is lost forever, however mitigating conditions can set this to be a specific period, but no less than 5 years. The rights are lost from the day the judgement is final. If the loss is during a specific period, it starts from that day the penalty is finished. If special conditions are met, rehabilitation can be granted by law. The conditions of Civil Penal Code § 79 cannot be used on actions, which are judged by this law.

§7. The responsibility to serve the sentence according to this law, as well as completing all parts of the judgment, cannot become obsolete.

Grafenwöhr barracks in southern Germany. (Photo: Private)

The Officers' Mess at Grafenwöhr barracks. (Photo: Private)

Grafenwöhr barracks, where *Freikorps Danmark* was abolished in 1943. (Photo: Private)

A photograph taken from a balloon of Grafenwöhr barracks in southern Germany. (Photo: Private)

Officers of the volunteer Danish *SS* soldiers of the Replacement Company who arrived at Grafenwöhr in 1943. (Photo: Henrik Asferg)

250 volunteer Danish *SS* soldiers of the Replacement Company arrive at Grafenwöhr in 1943. (Photo: Henrik Asferg)

250 soldiers of the volunteer Danish *SS* Replacement Company arrive at Grafenwöhr in 1943. (Photo: Henrik Asferg)

The volunteer Danish *SS* soldiers of the Replacement Company get in line at Grafenwöhr in 1943. (Photo: Henrik Asferg)

Officers and men of the Replacement Company march through Grafenwöhr in 1943. (Photo: Henrik Asferg)

Some of the 250 volunteer Danish *SS* soldiers of the Replacement Company march into Grafenwöhr in 1943. (Photo: Henrik Asferg)

General Felix Steiner arrives at the parade at Grafenwöhr on 20 May 1943. (Photo: Henrik Asferg)

General Felix Steiner takes the salute as he arrives at the parade at Grafenwöhr on 20 May 1943. (Photo: Henrik Asferg)

The *SS* Music Corps at the parade at Grafenwöhr on 20 May 1943. (Photo: Henrik Asferg)

The *SS* Music Corps performs at the parade at Grafenwöhr on 20 May 1943. (Photo: Henrik Asferg)

The *SS* Music Corps at the parade at Grafenwöhr on 20 May 1943. (Photo: Henrik Asferg)

The *SS* Music Corps at the parade at Grafenwöhr on 20 May 1943. (Photo: Henrik Asferg)

The parade at Grafenwöhr on 20 May 1943. (Photo: Henrik Asferg)

Men and officers in the parade at Grafenwöhr on 20 May 1943. (Photo: Henrik Asferg)

Another shot of the parade at Grafenwöhr on 20 May 1943. (Photo: Henrik Asferg)

A close-up shot of soldiers taking part in the parade at Grafenwöhr on 20 May 1943. (Photo: Henrik Asferg)

The parade at Grafenwöhr on 20 May 1943. (Photo: Henrik Asferg)

The men march during the parade at Grafenwöhr on 20 May 1943. (Photo: Henrik Asferg)

The men get in line for the parade at Grafenwöhr on 20 May 1943. (Photo: Henrik Asferg)

Straightening the ranks for the parade at Grafenwöhr on 20 May 1943. (Photo: Henrik Asferg)

Another photograph of the parade at Grafenwöhr on 20 May 1943. (Photo: Henrik Asferg)

The parade at Grafenwöhr on 20 May 1943. (Photo: Henrik Asferg)

Officers in discussion during the parade at Grafenwöhr on 20 May 1943. (Photo: Henrik Asferg)

A panoramic view of the parade at Grafenwöhr on 20 May 1943. (Photo: Henrik Asferg)

General Steiner hosted a dinner for envoy Mohr at the castle of Plassenburg on 27 July 1943. (Photo: Poul Christensen)

Envoy Carl Otto Mohr meets some of the men on 28 July 1943. (Photo: Henrik Asferg)

Envoy Carl Otto Mohr, with Hermegild Graf Von Westphalen on the right, on 28 July 1943. (Photo: Private)

Envoy Carl Otto Mohr, with (right) Hermegild Graf Von Westphalen and Poul Neergaard Jacobsen, on 28 July 1943. (Photo: Private)

Envoy Carl Otto Mohr in discussion with officers on 28 July 1943. (Photo: Private)

Trying to keep the soldiers in line when envoy Mohr and General Steiner visited on 28 July 1943. (Photo: Henrik Asferg)

Envoy Carl Otto Mohr discusses matters with Hermegild Graf Von Westphalen on 28 July 1943. (Photo: Private)

General Felix Steiner greeting the soldiers on 28 July 1943. (Photo: Henrik Asferg)

General Felix Steiner on 28 July 1943. (Photo: Private)

General Felix Steiner speaks with a soldier on 28 July 1943. (Photo: Private)

General Felix Steiner (in a light coloured coat) greets troops on 28 July 1943. (Photo: Private)

Magnus Moeller (left) relaxes with a fellow soldier. (Photo: Magnus Moeller)

Freddy Boerge Vilhelm Hansen (left) poses with an unknown soldier in front of a vehicle fitted with a loudspeaker on 28 July 1943. (Photo: Poul Christensen)

On the left is Nielsson, a tailor from Aarhus. Next to him is Pauli Peter Christian Joergensen, born on 3 January 1907 in Kolding. Joergensen was sentenced to five years in prison after the war. He was part of the Replacement Company of *Freikorps Danmark*, and later 7th Company of *Regiment 24 Denmark*. (Photo: Henrik Asferg)

A group of unknown Danish soldiers with a 5cm PaK38 anti-tank gun. (Photo: Magnus Moeller)

Four unknown Danish soldiers, one of whom is obviously musically-minded. (Photo: Magnus Moeller)

7

Commanders from 29 June 1941 to 20 May 1943 and photos and biographies of soldiers of *Freikorps Danmark*

The four commanders who served in *Freikorps Danmark*, 1941-1943

Christian Peder Kryssing.
Born on 7 July 1891 in Kolding, Denmark.
Died on 7 July 1976 in Haderslev, Denmark.

The first commander of *Freikorps Danmark* from 29 June 1941 to 22 February 1942. C.P. Kryssing was removed as commander, as he was not a convinced Nazi. After the war, he was imprisoned for eight years, which was reduced to four years after an appeal. The war was particularly tough on C.P. Kryssing, as both of his sons were killed on the Eastern Front, and his wife became seriously injured while serving as a nurse at the front in Tallinn, Estonia. He lost everything, and he had to live off handouts from his friends. Kryssing was bitter about the Danish system of justice for the rest of his life. See more pictures of C.P. Kryssing and his family in the appendix on page 395-398. (Photo: Jann Hornum)

Christian Frederik von Schalburg.
Born on 15 April 1906 in Zmeinogorsk, Russia.
Died on 2 June 1942 in Biakowo, Russia.

The second commander of *Freikorps Danmark* from 22 Fedbruary 1942 to 2 June 1942 was C.F. von Schalburg. He had a Russian mother and a Danish father. He was particularly popular and respected during his time as commander of *Freikorps Danmark*. He died during an attack on a Russian bridgehead at Biakowo in Russia. See another photo of C.F. von Schalburg on page 394. (Photo: Private)

Hans Albert Von Lettow-Vorbeck.
Born on 28 April 1901 in Berlin, Germany.
Died on 11 June 1942 at Bol. Dubowizy, Russia.

From 9-11 June 1942, Hans Albert Von Lettow-Vorbeck was the third commander of *Freikorps Danmark*. He only experienced a few days as commander of the *Freikorps* before he was killed during a counter-attack on the village of Bol. Dubowizy. (Photo: Private)

Knud Boerge Martinsen.
Born on 30 November 1905 in Sandved on Zealand, Denmark.
Died (executed) on 5 June 1949 in Copenhagen, Denmark.

The fourth and final commander of *Freikorps Danmark*, from 11 June 1942 to 20 May 1943, was K.B. Martinsen. After the abolition of *Freikorps Danmark*, he continued as leader of the Schalburg Corps in Denmark. After the war, he was executed for a civilian murder, which he had committed in Denmark during the war. (Photo: Private)

Photos/biographies of the soldiers of *Freikorps Danmark*

Joergen Eriksen.
Born on 9 July 1919 in Holm at Nordborg, Denmark.
Survived the war.

In 1941, Eriksen joined *Freikorps Danmark*. He was reported killed on 29 January 1944 in Russia in a death announcement in Danish newspaper *Faedrelandet*. However, he unexpectedly reappeared and was arrested at the border at Krusaa on 14 Novembet 1945. What happened during the interim is unknown. He was subsequently sentenced to two years in prison for actively serving in the war alongside the Germans, and lost all of his civilian rights. (Photo: Henrik Asferg)

Peter Bernhard Petersen.
Born on 17 March 1924 in Langaa at Randers, Denmark.
Died on 20 July 1942 at Biakowo, Russia.

Along with his commander, Heinz Henneke, Peter Bernhard Petersen was at the command post of *Freikorps Danmark* at Biakowo when a Russian shell hit nearby and fatally wounded the 18-year-old Petersen, who died during his transport to the camp hospital. Petersen, who belonged to 3rd Company of *Freikorps Danmark*, was buried at the town of Kostkowa in Russia. (Photo: Private)

Hans Peter Kjeld Andersen.
Born on 31 May 1913 in Praestoe, Denmark.
Died on 25 December 1943 at the camp hospital in Waulino, Russia.

Hans Peter Kjeld Andersen was fatally wounded by a shot to the head following the battles at Kondratowo/Laskaturina, from which he later died. He was a former reserve officer of the Danish armed forces, and belonged to the 1st Company of *Freikorps Danmark*. He received the Iron Cross 2nd Class for his actions in the Demyansk Pocket in 1942. (Photo: Private)

Evald Niels Hjalmar Vangebo.
Born on 22 August 1913 at Skuderloese in Naestved, Denmark.
Survived the war.

In July 1941, when he joined *Freikorps Danmark*, he was a warehouse worker, and was transferred to the Replacement Company of the *Freikorps*. His service during the war is unknown. However, he was arrested at his home on 6 May 1945, and was later sentenced to three years in prison and loss of all of his civil rights for five years. (Photo: Henrik Asferg)

Johannes Just Nielsen.
Born on 6 July 1920 in Darum at Esbjerg, Denmark
Died on 28 May 1942 at Ssutoki/Biakowo, Russia.

Johannes Just Nielsen was a reserve officer of the Danish armed forces as well as a part of the Danish Finland Battalion during the Finnish-Russian winter war of 1939-1940. He was mentioned as the first Dane in the *Ehrenblatt des Deutschen Heeres* newspaper. He belonged to the 1st Company of *Freikorps Danmark* at the time of his death, and his body was never found. He received a posthumous Iron Cross 2nd Class. (Photo: Private)

Martin Ingemann Bruun Olesen.
Born on 2 February 1914 in Rebild, Denmark.
Survived the war.

In June 1941, Martin Ingemann Bruun Olesen joined *Freikorps Danmark* and was a part of 1st Company. He served until the end of the war, and was arrested in Krusaa on 11 December 1945. He was later charged and punished by imprisonment for active German war duty. (Photo: Jann Hornum)

Carl Johan Wengel Lauritsen.
Born on 4 July 1923 in Aarhus, Denmark.
Died on 22 February 1943 at a camp hospital in Orscha, Russia.

He worked in Germany until he joined *Freikorps Danmark* in November 1941, where he belonged to 3rd Company. Carl Johan Wengel Lauritsen was sent to the camp hospital on 22 January 1943 after being shot in a lung. However, he died a month later due to pneumonia caused by his injury. (Photo: Per Beck Nielsen)

Knud Ernst Orla Christensen.
Born on 6 November 1914 in Copenhagen, Denmark.
Survived the war.

He was working as a greengrocer, but prior to this had worked in Germany, when he joined *Freikorps Danmark* on 20 August 1941 and became part of 1st Company. He caught malaria and was wounded by shrapnel in the Demyansk Pocket. He decided to withdraw from *Regiment 24 Denmark* in October 1943, and thereafter became a member of the Gestapo. On 5 January 1945 in Odense, he shot and killed a member of the resistance who had been arrested and handcuffed. He received a death sentence due to that action during the trials after the war. Later, this was reduced to a life sentence in prison, but he was pardoned and released on 30 May 1959. (Photo: Private)

Joergen Johannsen Noerskov.
Born on 2 June 1900 in Bedsted at Roedekro, Denmark.
Survived the war.

Joergen Johannsen Noerskov participated in the First World War on Germany's side, and was one of the first to volunteer for *Freikorps Danmark*. He received the Iron Cross 2nd Class in June 1942 in the Demyansk Pocket, where he was a part of 1st Company. Arrested on 10 May 1945, he was sentenced to four years in prison and loss of all civilian rights. (Photo: Private)

Christian Frederik Windrup Andersen.
Born on 26 September 1913 in Ubby at Holbaek, Denmark.
Survived the war.

In July 1941, he joined *Freikorps Danmark* and became a part of 1st Company. In September 1943, he returned home to Denmark, and for a while he joined the Schalburg Corps. From July 1944, he was a guard at *Shellhuset*, the Gestapo headquarters in Denmark, as part of the German *SD* (*Sicherheitsdienst*). Arrested on 6 May 1945, he was sentenced to four years in prison, which in May 1946 was reduced to two-and-a-half years. (Photo: Private)

Müller Nielsen.
Born on 28 April 1917 in Tolne, Denmark.
Reported missing at Kurland, Latvia, in January 1945.

In February 1942, Müller Nielsen joined *Freikorps Danmark*, where he was part of its Replacement Company. He was later a staff officer of *Regiment 24 Denmark*. During the battles in Latvia in 1945, he was reported missing. After the war, the family searched for him through the Red Cross, without success. (Photo: Private)

Johan Heinrich Knudsen.
Born on 29 January 1919 in Hoejbjerg at Viborg, Denmark.
Reported missing at Kurland, Latvia, on 28 January 1945.

On 7 July 1941, Knudsen joined *Freikorps Danmark*. Until the winter battles of 1942-1943, he was part of the Replacement Company, after which he became a staff officer of the *Freikorps*. When he was reported missing in Latvia in 1945, he was a part of the 13th Company of *Regiment 24 Denmark*. For his efforts in the war, he received the Iron Cross 1st and 2nd Class. His body was never found. (Photo: Private)

Per Soerensen.
Born on 31 May 1913 in Essenbaek at Randers, Denmark.
Died on 25 April 1945 in Berlin, Germany.

Per Soerensen was a legendary and highly decorated commander of *Freikorps Danmark*, and later *Regiment 24 Denmark*. He fought until the end of the war, and was injured at least seven times. However, Per Soerensen's luck ran out during the final days in Berlin in 1945, when he was fatally shot in the head. After the war, Per Soerensen's mother transferred the body of her son back to Denmark, and he is now buried at Loekken Church. (Photo: Private)

Magnus Moeller.
Born on 14 September 1920 in Tyrstrup at Kolding, Denmark.
Survived the war.

Magnus Moeller was part of 4th Company of *Freikorps Danmark*, but decided to leave the corps during the summer of 1943. He believed that he had signed up for a purely Danish *Freikorps*, and would not serve the *Waffen-SS* directly. After some struggle, Magnus Moeller had his contract cancelled and went home to Denmark. However, after the war his past caught up with him. Like many others, he was arrested and sentenced to prison and loss of his civil rights. (Photo: Magnus Moeller)

Kaj Enna.
Born on 30 September 1923 in Soeborg, Denmark.
Died on 25 February 1943 at Taidy, Russia.

Kaj Enna was one of C.F. von Schalburg's '*bloddrenge*' (Blood boys) from his time with the *NSU* (youth section of the Danish Nazi Party). During the battles of the Demyansk Pocket, he received the Iron Cross 2nd Class and was wounded. He worked at a bureau of the German *Wehrmacht* in Vanloese, Denmark, before he joined *Freikorps Danmark* during the summer of 1941, where he was part of 3rd Company. (Photo: Private)

Gerhardt Viggo Bentzen.
Born on 18 Ferbruary 1919 in Copenhagen, Denmark.
Died on 2 June 1942 at Biakowo, Russia.

Gerhardt Viggo Bentzen was also one of C.F. von Schalburg's '*bloddrenge*' from his time with the *NSU*. On 1 August 1941, he joined *Freikorps Danmark*. During the battles in the Demyansk Pocket, he was a part of 3rd Company. He died during the attack on the Russian bridgehead on 2 June 1942, when he and others tried to return the body of their commander, C.F. von Schalburg, to their own lines. (Photo: Private)

Boerge Preben Hern.
Born on 12 July 1921 in Copenhagen, Denmark.
Died on 23 November 1944 in Kurland, Latvia.

Boerge Preben Hern was another of C.F. von Schalburg's '*bloddrenge*', and on 5 August 1941, he joined *Freikorps Danmark*. He was attached to the 3rd Company, and received the Iron Cross 2nd Class following the battles at Taidy in Russia on 25 February 1943. When he died in Kurland, he was part of the 10th Company of *Regiment 24 Denmark*. (Photo: Private)

Carl Nielsen.
Born on 15 May 1920 in Slagelse, Denmark.
Survived the war.

Carl Nielsen was an trained tailor, but joined *Freikorps Danmark*. Later, he became *Rottenführer* in the 6th Company of *Regiment 24 Denmark*. Like all the other *Waffen-SS* volunteers, he was punished by prison and loss of civilian rights for five years. After the war, he resumed working as a tailor. He died in 2003. (Photo: Private)

Axel Graabaek.
Born on 19 May 1911 in Herning, Denmark.
Died on 22 April 1943 in Fredericia, Denmark, at a war hospital.

Having previously served in the Danish Army,, he joined *Freikorps Danmark* on 20 July 1941. He was a part of the staff of officers attached to the pioneer platoon of the *Freikorps*. He was severely injured in the Demyansk Pocket, and in April 1943 died of these wounds at a hospital in Denmark. He received the Iron Cross 2nd Class for his actions at Demyansk. (Photo: Private)

Helge Gunnar Mortensen.
Born on 24 May 1922 in Haslev, Denmark.
Survived the war.

On 14 July 1941, Helge Gunnar Mortensen joined *Freikorps Danmark*, and travelled to its base in Hamburg on 9 August. He became part of the Staff Company of *Freikorps Danmark*, and later joined *Regiment 24 Denmark*. After the war, he was at the Albertsdorf camp at Flensburg, and on 10 December 1945 was transferred to Denmark, where he was sentenced to prison for 18 months in February 1946, as well as losing all civilian rights. (Photo: Private)

Alfred Jonstrup.
Born on 2 November 1916 in Frederikshavn, Denmark.
Survived the war, but as a heavily disabled soldier.

On 15 August 1941, he joined *Freikorps Danmark*, and became part of 3rd Company during the battles in the Demyansk Pocket, where he received the Iron Cross 2nd Class. He was mentioned in *Ehrenblatt des Deutschen Heeres* in 1944, as his jaw was shot off while serving with *Regiment 24 Denmark* during the battles in Kurland. Despite his grave injury, he continued his duty, receiving the Iron Cross 1st Class. After the war, he was sentenced to four years in prison, which was reduced to one year. After this, he became a night porter at a hotel in Copenhagen, but made few public appearances due to his jaw injury. (Photo: Private)

Jens Andreas Kristensen.
Born on 10 April 1913 in Vester Thorup, Denmark.
Died on 5 March 1944 at Siivertsi, Estonia.

Prior to joining *Freikorps Danmark* on 7 July 1941, he was a dragoon of the royal household troops. He was a part of the first team of volunteers who went to Hamburg, Germany, on 19 July 1941. He became part of 3rd Company, and was wounded at the Demyansk Pocket in 1942. After the abolition of *Freikorps Danmark* in 1943, he joined the 2nd Company of *Regiment 24 Denmark*, and received the Iron Cross 2nd Class in the autumn of 1943. He was severely injured during the battles at Siivertsi in March 1944, and subsequently died of his wounds. (Photo: Knud Guldhammer Kristensen)

Svend Aage Jensen.
Born on 1 June 1920 in Svaerdborg, Denmark.
Survived the war.

In 1941, Svend Aage Jensen joined *Freikorps Danmark*, and travelled to Hamburg on 19 July. He became part of 3rd Company of the *Freikorps*, and later joined *Regiment 24 Denmark*. Arrested in 1946, he was sentenced to 15 months in prison and loss of all civilian rights for five years. In 1985, Svend Aage Jensen wrote the book *Svaerdborg fortaeller* (*Svaerdborg tells*). (Photo: Bogans Forlag)

Iver Schmidt.
Born on 7 December 1907 in Daler, Denmark.
Died on 28 August 1944 in Narva, Estonia.

In June 1941, Iver Schmidt joined *Freikorps Danmark*, and was among the first group who went to Langenhorn barracks in Germany. He received the Iron Cross during the summer of 1942 for his efforts in the Demyansk Pocket. After the abolition of *Freikorps Danmark* in 1943, he joined *Regiment 24 Denmark*. Iver Schmidt died on 28 August 1944 near the border town of Narva, Estonia. (Photo: Poul Christensen)

Olaf Jakob Boyesen Friis.
Born on 20 September 1914 in Vesterland, Denmark.
Survived the war.

In 1941, he joined *Freikorps Danmark*, serving with the 3rd Company. For his efforts at Velikije Luki, he received the Iron Cross 2nd Class on 11 January 1943. After the abolition of *Freikorps Danmark*, he joined the staff of *Regiment 24 Denmark* with the rank of *Rottenführer*. He was wounded at the advanced observation post of *Regiment 24 Denmark* at Dolgaja Niva, Russia, on 8 July 1944. After the war, he was sentenced to jail and loss of all civilian rights for five years. (Photo: Poul Christensen)

Freddy Boerge Vilhelm Hansen.
Born on 3 January 1914 in Copenhagen, Denmark.
Survived the war.

Freddy Boerge Vilhelm Hansen joined *Freikorps Danmark* on 15 August 1941. He participated in the battles at the Demyansk Pocket and Velikije Luki. After the abolition of *Freikorps Danmark* in 1943, he served with *Regiment 24 Denmark*. After the war, he was sentenced to 18 months in prison and loss of all civilian rights for five years. (Photo: Poul Christensen)

Andreas Mortensen.
Born on 29 June 1921 in Toender, Denmark.
Survived the war.

Andreas Mortensen most likely joined *Freikorps Danmark* late in the summer of 1941. He was part of the staff of the Danish volunteers, and received the Iron Cross 2nd Class on 2 August 1942. After *Freikorps Danmark* was abolished, he joined *Regiment 24 Denmark*. During the battles in Budapest in 1945, he lost an eye. After the war, he was sentenced to five years in prison and loss of all civilian rights. (Photo: Poul Christensen)

Egon Koch.
Born on 12 May 1921 in Hadsund, Denmark.
Survived the war.

During the summer of 1941, Egon Koch joined *Freikorps Danmark* and became part of 3rd Company. After the abolition of the *Freikorps*, he joined *Regiment 24 Denmark* and received the Iron Cross 2nd Class on 20 February 1944. He was wounded twice on the Eastern Front; the first time on 6 August 1944 at Narva, Estonia, and then on 23 September 1944 at Lidikas, Latvia. After the war, Egon Koch was punished with jail and a loss of all civilian rights. (Photo: Poul Christensen)

Kaj Bertramsen.
Born on 13 February 1913 in Berlin, Germany.
Died on 29 July 1944 at Kinderheimhöhe, Estonia.

Before the war, Kaj Bertramsen was an officer of the reserve of the Danish armed forces. He joined *Freikorps Danmark* in July 1941, and was subsequently appointed leader of the replacement troops until December 1942. He then decided to join the winter battles at Velikije Luki in Russia as a part of 3rd Company of the *Freikorps*. After *Freikorps Danmark* was disbanded, he was for a time commander of 6th Company of *Regiment 24 Denmark*. On 27 July 1944, he became commander of 11th Company of *Regiment 24 Denmark*. He was killed two days later, and his body was never found. On 20 February 1944, he had received the Iron Cross 2nd Class. (Photo: Private)

Svend Arne Larsen.
Born on 10 September 1921 in Klithuse, Denmark.
Survived the war.

Svend Arne Larsen joined *Freikorps Danmark* on the 2 July 1941, and participated in the battles at the Demyansk Pocket. On 23 July 1942, he was severely injured in the shoulder from a shot from a Russian sniper. After a stay at the camp hospital, Svend Arne Larsen was judged as fit for combat, and was transferred to *Regiment 24 Denmark*, and became a part of 7th Company. On 10 September 1944 in Latvia, he was injured once again, this time by a piece of shrapnel in his right forearm. For the rest of the war, Svend Arne Larsen was resting. He was arrested at his parents' farm on 8 May 1945, and sentenced to prison for three years as well as a loss of all civilian rights for five years. (Photo: Frants Jensen Langhoff)

Vagn Oest.
Born on 24 December 1920 in Randers, Denmark.
Died on 31 October 1944 in Aarhus, Denmark.

Before joining *Freikorps Danmark* on 14 July 1941, Vagn Oest was a carpenter. He participated in the battles at the Demyansk Pocket and Velikije Luki in Russia. For his efforts at the Demyansk Pocket, he received the Iron Cross 2nd Class. After the abolishment of *Freikorps Danmark*, he became a part of the 11th Company of *Regiment 24 Denmark*. In July 1944, at Narva, Estonia, he was severely wounded and was transferred to the camp hospital. Following this, he went home on a sick leave. He was at the Gestapo headquarters at Aarhus University, when he died during a bombing raid by the Royal Air Force on 31 October 1944. He achieved the rank of *Unterscharführer* for German war duty. (Photo: Peter Nybye Oest)

Niels Martinus Larsen.
Born on 23 July 1920 in Goerding, Denmark.
Died in 1987.

Niels Martinus Larsen joined *Freikorps Danmark* in July 1941, and was among the first to arrive at Langenhorn barracks in Hamburg. He was a part of 3rd Company. On 15 November 1941, he was sent to the *SS-Pioneer-Ersatz-Battalion* school in Dresden to be trained. He continued in *Regiment 24 Denmark* in 1943. However, he deserted in April 1944, but was eventually caught by the Gestapo and spend some time in a jail in Hamburg, before he was transferred to the Neuengammen camp. He was handed over to the Danish authorities after the war, where he was sentenced to one year in jail and a loss of all of his civilian rights. Following this, Niels Martinus Larsen moved to Sweden. (Photo: Frants Jensen Langhoff)

Jens Effersoe Kryssing.
Born on 28 June 1924 in Holbaek, Denmark.
Missing in action in Russia on 28 May 1942.

The youngest son of the Commander, C.P. Kryssing, Jens Effersoee Kryssing joined *Freikorps Danmark* on 12 July 1941. When his father was removed as commander of *Freikorps Danmark* in 1942, and transferred to another unit, Jens Effersoee Kryssing was also transferred to another *SS* unit, *Division Totenkopf.* With this new unit, he was severely wounded and had to be left behind. He was later reported missing at the village of Kirillowschtshina (at Lake Ilmen) in Russia on 28 May 1942. His body has never been found. C.P. Kryssing wrote many letters to the Red Cross in Germany in the years following the war, in the hope of news about his son's fate on the Eastern Front, but this was in vain. (Photo: Jann Hornum)

Magnus Mikkelsen.
Born on 16 January 1920 in Agersted, Denmark.
Died in 2016.

Magnus Mikkelsen was adventurous, so he got on a train for Copenhagen and went to the first recruitment office to join *Freikorps Danmark*. He participated in the battles in the Demyansk Pocket, where he was severely injured, being shot through a lung. After a long stay away from the front due to his injury, he did not want to participate in the war again, as he had realized that war was dangerous, and the Russians shot to kill. Instead, he became a railway guard for the German occupation troops in Denmark. It was for this that he was sentenced to 12 years in jail. However, he was relatively quickly released. (Photo: Private)

Knud Per Dahl Nielsen.
Born on 6 March 1918 in Hoeng, Denmark.
Died on 13 February 1944 in Narva, Estonia.

Knud Per Dahl Nielsen joined *Freikorps Danmark* on 2 August 1941, and became a part of 1st Company. He was wounded during the battles at the Demyansk Pocket on 24 May 1942, and received the Iron Cross on 26 May 1942. After some recovery time, he returned to 1st Company through the Replacement Company of *Freikorps Danmark*. He also participated in the battles at Velikije Luki. When *Freikorps Danmark* was abolished in 1943, he became a part of 1st Company of *Regiment 24 Denmark*. Knud Per Dahl Nielsen was a part of a reconnaissance unit, when he was killed by a shot to the head on 13 February 1944 north of Narva, as *Oberscharführer* in *SS-Regiment 24 Denmark*. His body has never been found. (Photo: Rigborg Dahl Nielsen)

Appendix I

Insignia and Pay of the *Waffen-SS*

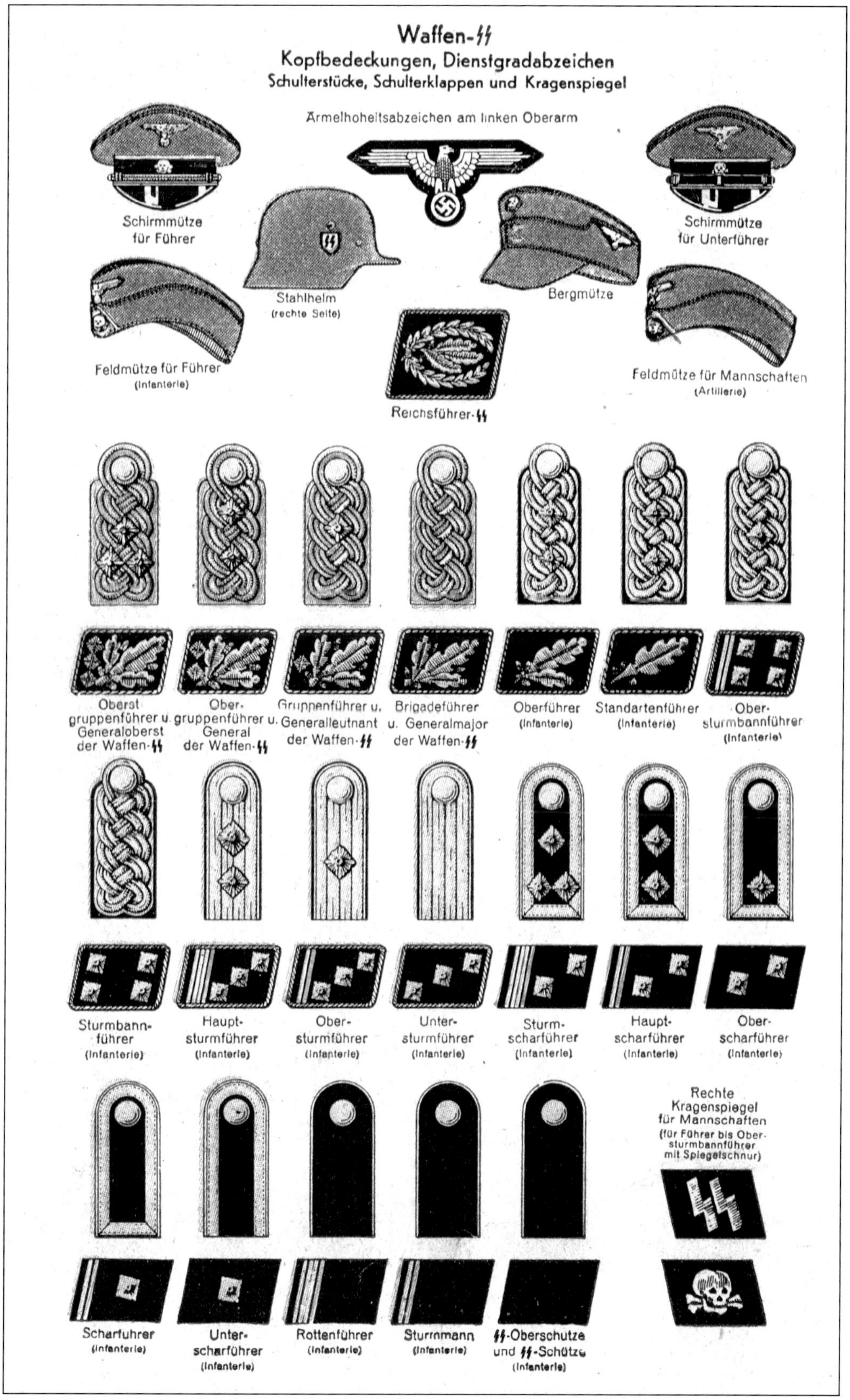

(Photo: Private)

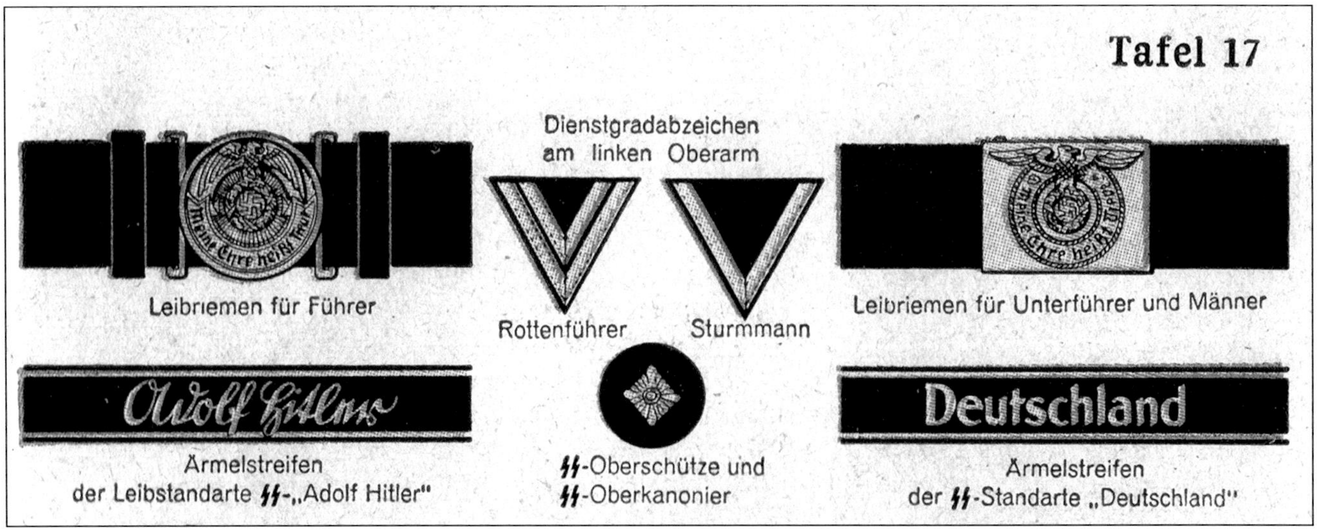

(Photo: Private)

Pay for volunteering Danes in *Freikorps Danmark* in 1942

Danske ϟϟ-Frivilliges Lønninger

Tjenestegrad	Wehr-sold-gruppe	ugift RM	ugift Kr.	gift RM	gift Kr.
Untersturmf.	10	210,—	402,30	270,—	517,24
Hauptscharf.	11	145,—	277,78	210,—	402,30
Sta-Oberjunker	—	—	—	—	—
Oberscharf.	12	140,—	268,20	205,—	392,72
Scharf.	13	130,—	249,04	185,—	354,41
Standartenjunker	—	—	—	—	—
Unterscharf.	14	105,—	201,15	145,—	277,78
ϟϟ-Junker	—	—	—	—	—
Rottenführer	15	75,—	143,68	105,—	201,15

For hver Barn under 16 Aar ydes et Børnetillæg paa RM 18,—.

One Danish *Kr.* in 1942 is about 10 British pence in 2017. RM = *Reichsmark*. (Photo: Private)

Appendix II

The Structure & Weapons of *Freikorps Danmark*

1. The Staff Company with an attached radio unit, workshop section, ammunition section, medical section and provisioning section.
2. 1st, 2nd and 3rd Company, which all had a rifleman unit as well as a mortar unit with two 81mm mortars.
3. 4th Company (the Heavy Company) had four 75mm infantry cannon, heavy machine guns and an anti-tank unit with three 50mm anti-tank guns.

Commanders of *Freikorps Danmark* in the Demyansk Pocket, 1942
C.F. von Schalburg (until 2 June), Hans Albert Von Lettow-Vorbeck (9-11 June), K.B. Martinsen (from 11 June).

Company commanders in the Demyansk Pocket, 1942
1st Company, *Obersturmführer* Per Soerensen.
2nd Company, *Obersturmführer* Harald Boy Hansen.
3rd Company, *Obersturmführer* Poul Neergaard.
4th Company, *Hauptsturmführer* K.B. Martinsen (until 11 June).

Commander of *Freikorps Danmark* at Velikije Luki in 1942-1943
K.B. Martinsen.

Company commanders at Velikije Luki in 1942-1943
1st Company, *Obersturmführer* Per Soerensen.
2nd Company, *Obersturmführer* Bent Worsoe Larsen.
3rd Company, *Obersturmführer* Heinz Henneke.
4th Company, *Obersturmführer* Helmut Stenger.

The weapons of *Freikorps Danmark*

Carbine 98 K: Shooting range about 300 metres, loaded with five rounds.
Parabellum 08 (Luger): Shooting range about 100 metres, magazine containing eight rounds.
MP 38, 40: Shooting range about 200 metres, rate of fire about 400 shots per minute.
MP 28: Shooting range about 50 metres, magazine containing 32 rounds.
MG-34: Shooting range about 1,830 metres with bipod, cartridge belt containing 50 rounds.
MG-42: Shooting range about 4,570 metres with tripod, cartridge belt containing 50 rounds.

Heavy weapons

81mm mortars: Shooting range about 1,900 meters, rate of fire 15 shots per minute.
50mm anti-tank gun: Shooting range about 200-300 metres.
75mm infantry gun: Shooting range about 3,500 metres.

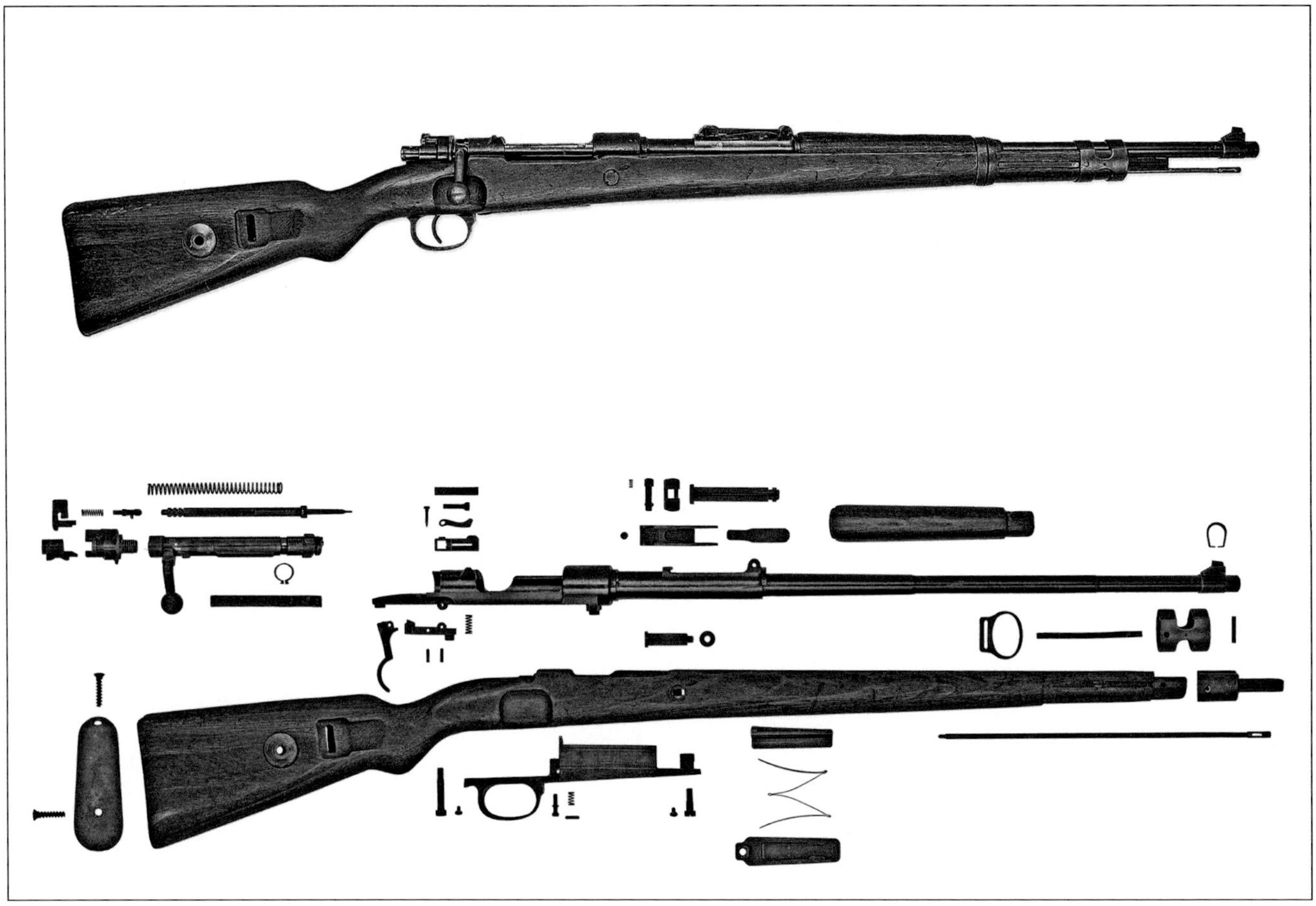

A German Carbine 98 K. (Photo: Private)

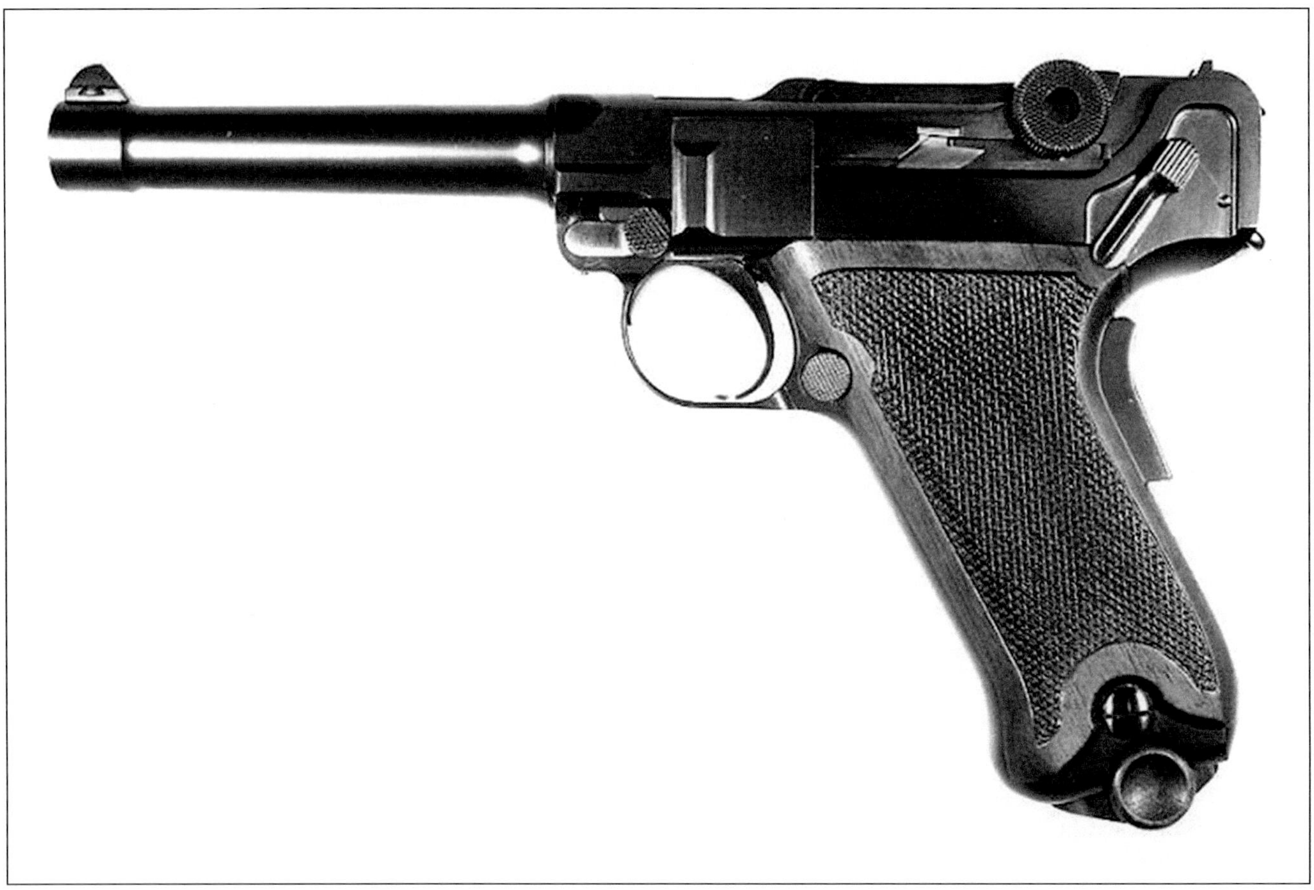

A German Luger. (Photo: Private)

A German MP. 38. (Photo: Private)

A German MG-34 with tripod. (Photo: Private)

A German MG-42 with bipod. (Photo: Private)

A German 81mm mortar. (Photo: Private)

Appendix III

Back to the Eastern Front with Magnus Moeller October 2014

Participants:

1. **Magnus Moeller**
2. **A Russian guide, Sergej Petrov**
3. **Hanne Lillie**
4. **Finn Andersen**
5. **A Russian interpreter, Inna Vinogradova**
6. **Niels Birger Danielsen**
7. **Bax Lindhardt**
8. **Jens Pank Bjerregaard**
9. **Lars Larsen**

The authors of this book have made multiple visits to the old Second World War battlefields on the Eastern Front, primarily Estonia, Lithuania and the area around St Petersburg (the former Leningrad) in Russia. However, the desire to travel to the area in which *Freikorps Danmark* fought fiercely in 1942 has always been great. Therefore, in summer 2014, we decided to travel to the battlefield locations, which are about 350km south of St Petersburg. Both of us have good relations with surviving *Freikorps Danmark* veteran Magnus Moeller. We therefore asked him if he wanted to join in our visit to the old battlefields, where he fought with *Freikorps Danmark* in the summer of 1942. We did not expect him to agree: Magnus was 94 years old, but still in astoundingly good psychological and physical shape for his age. However, to our surprise, he said yes. After that, we just had to plan the trip to the Eastern Front with the old Danish veteran.

We decided that the visit to Russia should last five days, consisting of two days travelling there and back, and three days in the field. The three days in Russia were planned as follows:

Day 1: Travelling from the small village of Vasilevschina to the former village of Biakowo, which no longer exists, as it was razed to the ground during the fierce battles in the summer of 1942. The distance was about 5km.

Day 2: Travelling from Vasilevschina to the bridgehead where C.F. von Schalburg, commander of *Freikorps Danmark*, fell on 2 June 1942. The distance from Vasilevschina is about 10km, in particularly swampy and frozen Russian terrain.

Day 3: Travelling to the old Russian village of Bol. Dubowizy, where *Freikorps Danmark* fought and suffered heavy losses in June, July and August 1942. Bol. Dubowizy was also razed during the battles, and the only surviving remains of the village are mortar holes and old war relics. Bol. Dubowizy lies about 5km north of Vasilevschina.

Visa

First, we had to settle a lot of practical stuff. It is difficult to enter Russia. The airplane tickets were easy to book, but you have to get a visa to travel there, and Russia is not an easy country to enter. A lot of paperwork had to be done, and everything had to be 100 percent correct, or else the visa would be rejected instantly. Sadly, this happened for us several times, but eventually we succeeded. Participants on the trip were the authors of this book, Magnus Moeller and two of our friends, Finn Andersen and Hanne Lillie. The latter both had a great interest in Danes who participated in the Second World War alongside the Germans, and enjoyed travelling to places which are difficult to reach.

Interpreter and guide

We needed a guide and an interpreter. Through various channels, we succeeded in finding the Russian Sergej Petrov, who lived in Vasilevschina and wanted to be our guide. We also found an interpreter, Inna Vinogradova, who spoke English at a sufficient level to help us. Sergej Petrov also had a tractor, which could take us across the muddy terrain in the area where *Freikorps Danmark* fought in 1942.

From the left: Jens Pank Bjerregaard, Sergej Petrov, Lars Larsen, Inna Vinogradova, Niels B. Danielsen, Hanne Lillie, Finn Andersen and Magnus Moeller. (Photo: Bax Lindhardt)

Travelling to Russia

We picked up Magnus Moeller at his home and drove to the airport in Billund, Denmark. The flight to St Petersburg was via Frankfurt in Germany. Fortunately, there were no problems concerning passports and visas etc. when we arrived in Russia. As agreed, the interpreter met us at the airport. Thereafter, we got our rental cars and headed south to the town of Staraya Russa, where we had booked a hotel for our stay in Russia. It was a long trip on poor Russian country roads, but we reached the town safely. We had booked a hotel in advance, and feared for the quality of it. However, it turned out to be a decent hotel by Russian standards.

Our home during the trip – Hotel *Polist* in Staraya Russa. (Photo: Private)

The tractor and trailer of Sergej Petrov in front of his house in the village of Vasilevschina, Russia. (Photo: Private)

Day 1

After a good night's sleep at the Russian hotel, followed by a solid breakfast, it was time to travel to Vasilevschina. There we were to meet our Russian guide, who lived about 70km from our hotel. While the Russian country roads had been poor the previous day, they now became very, very poor: a mix of stone, gravel, asphalt and deep holes. However, the worst part had to be the other Russian drivers, who all drove as if they never had any driving instruction. The address of our guide Sergej Petrov was simple: the first white house on the right hand side in Vasilevschina! As we reached our destination, late due to the conditions of the roads, Sergej had already made his tractor and trailer ready for the trip from Vasilevschina to Biakowo. We knew in advance that he did not have a new tractor: it was an old, sturdy model from the Soviet era, a *Vladimirs* from 1977. Still, it came as a bit of a surprise when we saw the tractor for the first time. It had no spring suspension, no lights and no license plate. The trailer was very small, with huge holes in it. There was just a small wooden plank across the front of the trailer to sit on. Other than that, the trailer was lined with hay. However, we took it all with a smile, and were excited to go on a trip to Biakowo by the old German '*Rullebane*', which *Freikorps Danmark* defended in summer 1942.

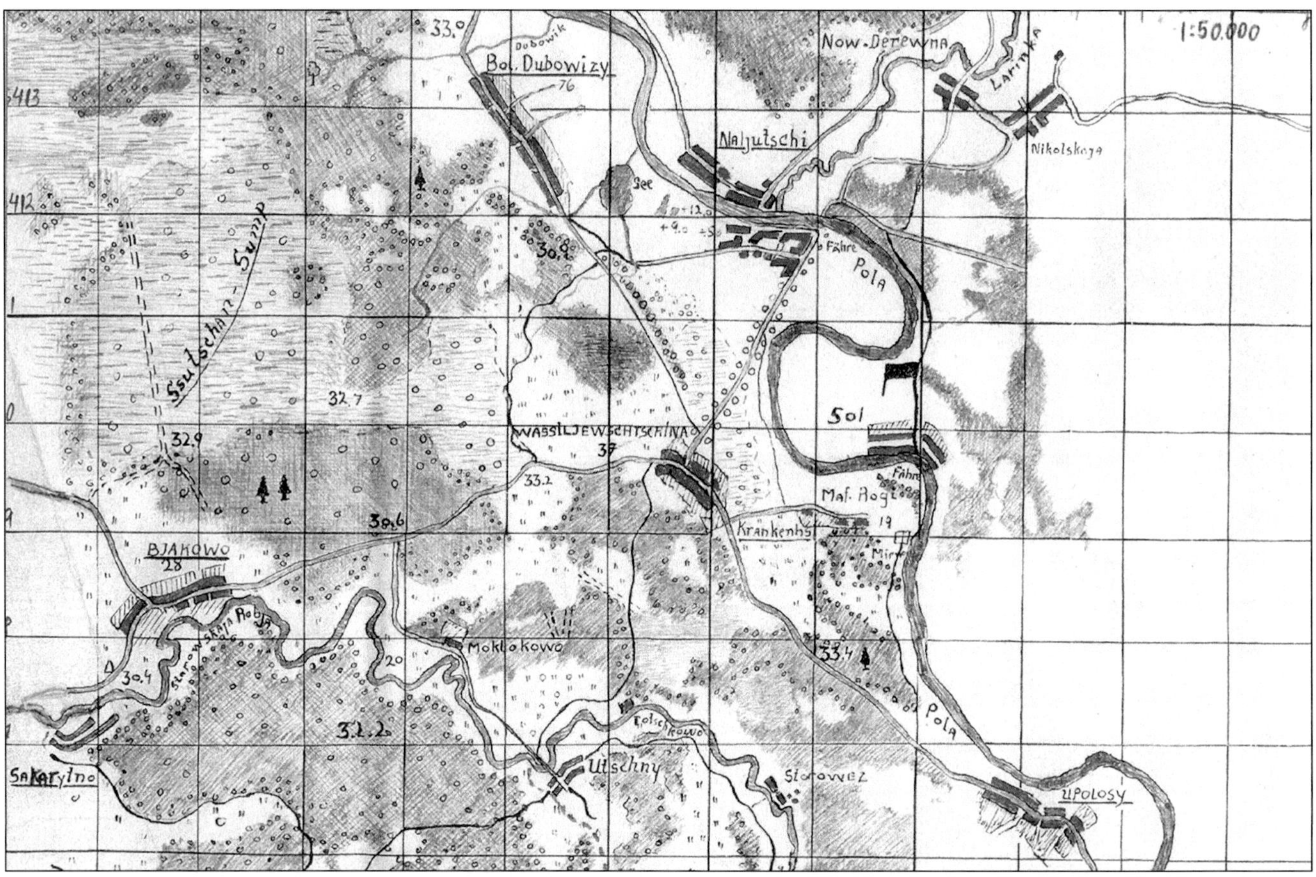

An old German war map depicting the area in which *Freikorps Danmark* fought in 1942. We drove the route (about 5km) from Vasilevschina to Biakowo via the old German '*Rullebanen*'. (Photo: Private)

Early frost and mud

Despite it only being the end of October, winter was already evident, with a hard frost. The sun was shining, but it was still about minus 14 degrees, so we knew we were facing a cold trip through the Russian forests. Most of us had not expected it to be this cold, however, so we had borrowed some warm blankets from our hotels, which we really needed on our trip. Under normal circumstances, the area is infamous for its muddy and impassable roads, and during the summer an unimaginable number of mosquitos. The Danes of *Freikorps Danmark* referred to the area as '*Myggedalen*' (the valley of mosquitos). Many of the volunteer Danish soldiers even thought that the mosquitos were worse than the Russians. However, all this mud was almost frozen, and had become a mixture of ice and almost impassable mud. It made the trip with the tractor especially tough, as it was like driving through a newly ploughed field which had frozen solid.

The old German *'Rullebanen'* at Vasilevschina, which is still there after more than 70 years. (Photo: Private)

From the left: Lars Larsen, Inna Vinogradova, Finn Andersen and Magnus Moeller. (Photo: Private)

The old German '*Rullebanen*' at Vasilevschina was filled with ice and mud, and was difficult to pass along. (Photo: Private)

Old war debris was strewn around the '*Rullebanen*', including this Russian helmet. (Photo: Private)

At Biakowo

Following a couple of hours driving, with some stops to look at old shell holes and material from the war, which is still strewn across the area, we reached the few remains of the small village of Biakowo. In 1942, it was at the centre of the battles to keep the '*Rullebanen*' open, allowing the Germans to transport forces in and out of the Demyansk Pocket. It had been a cold trip, especially for Magnus Moeller, so we quickly made a fire so he could get warm. However, before you start a fire in an old battlefield on the Eastern Front, you have to use a metal detector to check for grenades, shells etc. Finn Andersen used his metal detector in the area where we were planning to make a fire to get warm, cook and brew some much-needed coffee. We got the water for the coffee from the Robja stream, which ran about 25 metres from our fire. We spent some hours in the area and found a lot of old shells and other war scrap. Besides that, we saw the scars which the war had left, including shell holes and trenches, before we returned to Vasilevschina.

Finn Andersen scanning the ground with a metal detector, searching for war relics. (Photo: Private)

Our guide, Sergej Petrov, started a fire so Magnus Moeller could get warm in the cold weather. (Photo: Private)

The authors of this book enjoying a cup of coffee made with water from the Robja stream at Biakowo. (Photo: Private)

The Robja stream at Biakowo on a beautiful cold day in October 2014. (Photo: Private)

The water of the Robja stream had a weird, brown colour, but it tasted remarkably good in our coffee. (Photo: Private)

We left the '*Rullebanen*' and had to drive 5km in dense Russian forest and swamp. (Photo: Private)

Day 2

The first day's trip had been so hard on Magnus Moeller that we did not believe he could stand another tough day of driving through the Russian forests by tractor. On the second day, we had to travel twice as far to reach the area in which *Freikorps Danmark* fought on 2 June 1942. That was the day when C.F. von Schalburg fell, along with many other Danish volunteer soldiers. We agreed with Magnus that he would stay at Sergej Petrov's house, and Mrs Petrov promised to take good care of him. Hanne Lillie also felt a bit ill, and decided to stay with Magnus. For the rest of us, a difficult journey lay ahead. The first 5km were the same as the day before, whereafter we had to leave the '*Rullebanen*' and drive in the Russian forest for the last 5km. Sergej, our guide, had warned us that it would be a tough trip, and that we most likely would encounter some problems along the way: his prediction was true. We travelled the first 5km without any trouble; however, as we entered the forest, the terrain became much more difficult. Fortunately, Sergej had brought a chainsaw, and at times we literally had to cut our way through the forest.

Stuck

As we entered the dense forest, the ground was not nearly as frozen, which meant mud, deep puddles and problems. The tractor was stuck several times, but each time Sergej managed to get it free of the mud. He was skilled at using the hoisting mechanism at the back of the tractor, but each time we were stuck, we lost some time, which was starting to be an issue. We had to get back again at some point. However, after hours of struggle, we reached the bridgehead at which *Freikorps Danmark* fought and suffered severe casualties on 2 June 1942. The place is used from time to time, as a shelter is placed in a tree, which is most likely used by Russians who are looking for something they can sell. There was still a lot of war debris, helmets etc. Russian memorial plaques have been placed on some of the trees. Other than that, it is unimaginably desolate and very quiet. We start talking about how weird it was, to be at the exact spot where battles in the Second World War were taking place more than 70 years ago, and where many young Danish men had to give up their life because they decided to dress in Hitler's uniforms. After a couple of hours at the spot, we returned without problems back to Vasilevschina.

The authors of this book stuck along with the tractor in the Russian swamp. (Photo: Bax Lindhardt)

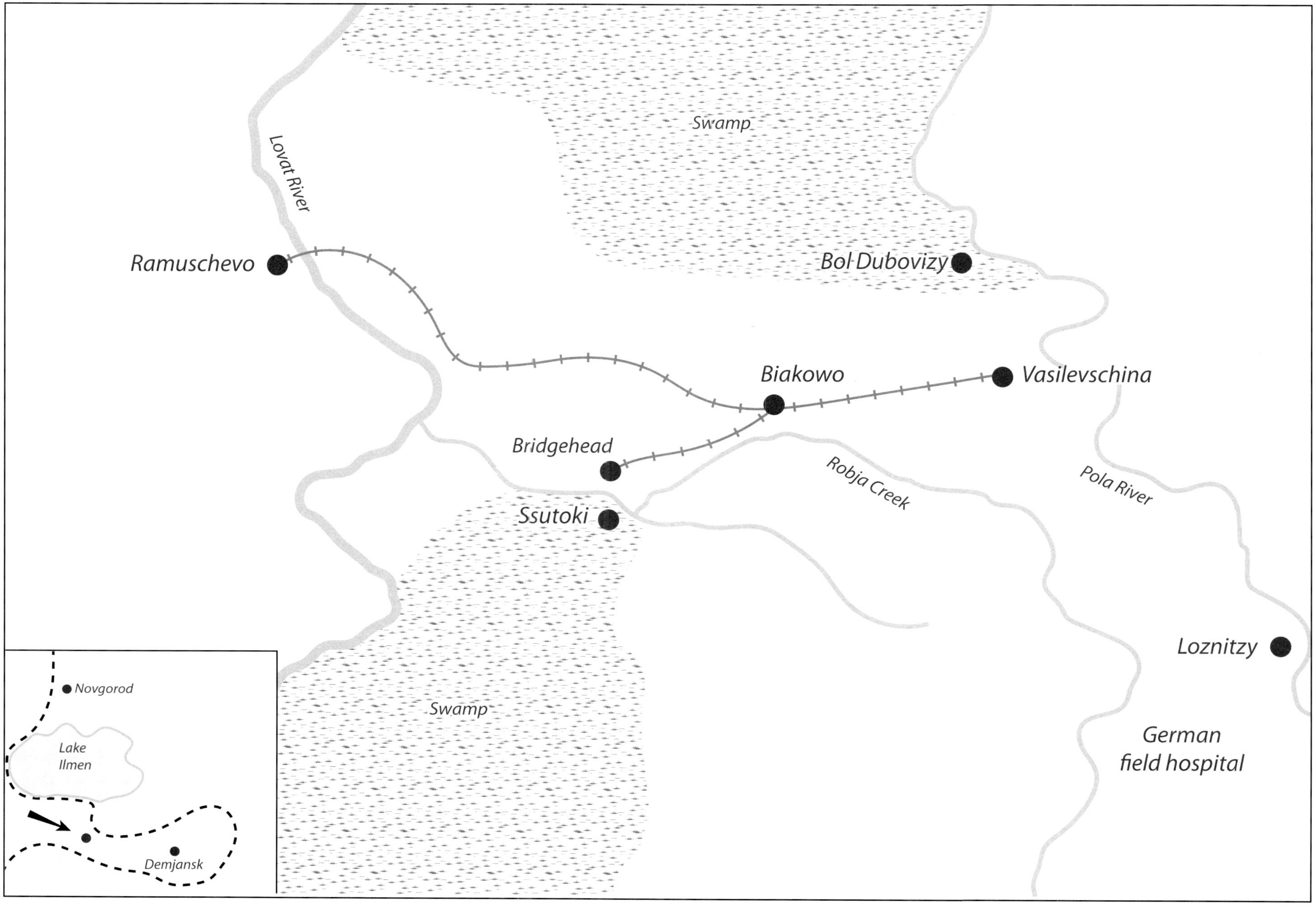

Day 2. Our trip from Vasilevschina to the Russian bridgehead was about 10 km. (Map by George Anderson based on sketch by Lasse Larsen)

Yet again, we were stuck in the Russian mud. (Photo: Bax Lindhardt)

War debris is still strewn around the place where C.F. von Schalburg fell on 2 June 1942. (Photo: Private)

Russian descendants have put up memorial plates to those who fell on the trees at the bridgehead. (Photo: Private)

A view of the bridgehead where C.F. von Schalburg was killed on 2 June 1942. (Photo: Private)

Another view of the bridgehead where C.F. von Schalburg was killed. (Photo: Private)

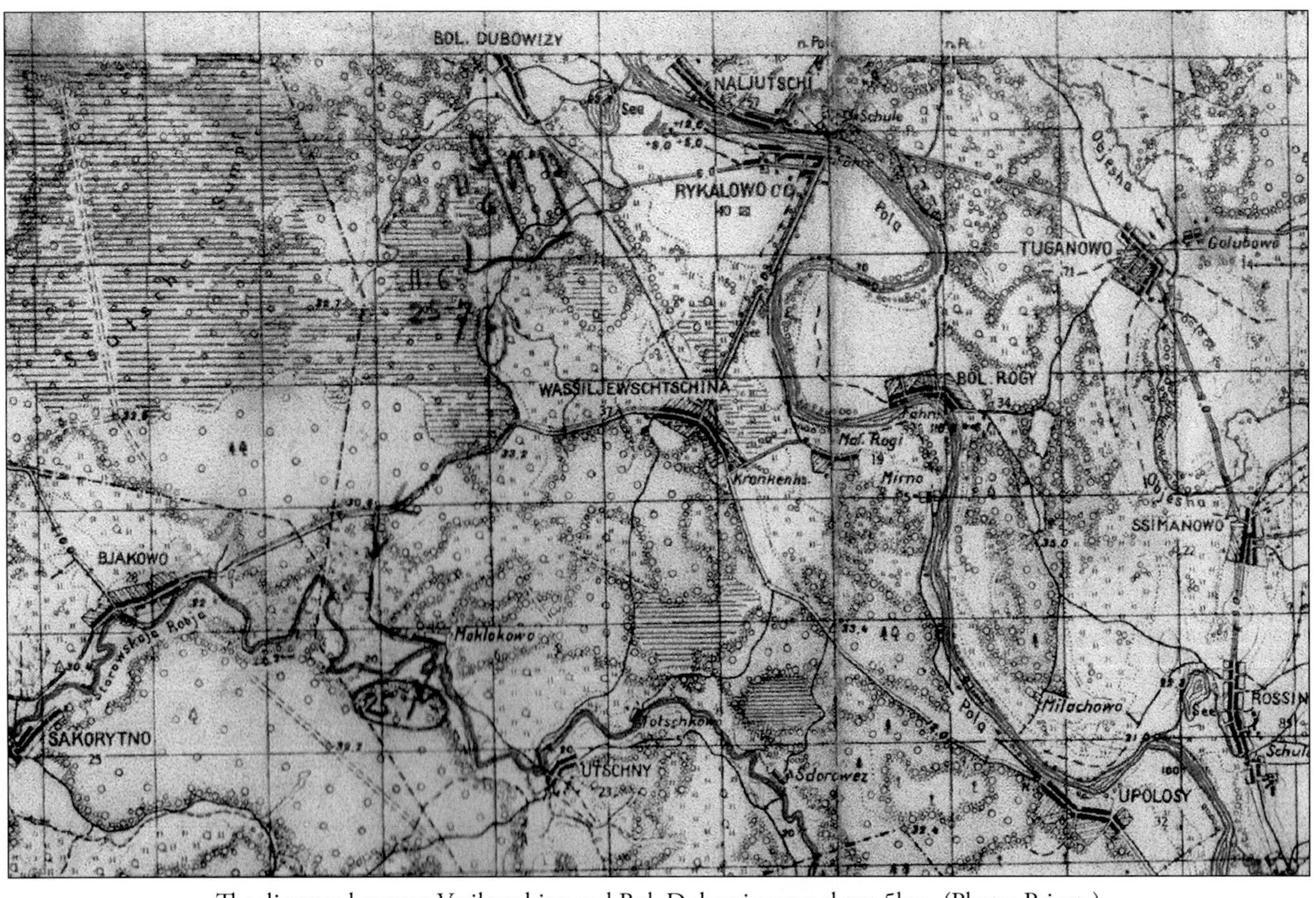

The distance between Vasilevschina and Bol. Dubowizy was about 5km. (Photo: Private)

Day 3

The trip on the third day was towards the village of Bol. Dubowizy, which lies about 5km north of Vasilevschina. The village was the location of fierce battles during the summer of 1942, when the stretch between the two villages was the only place in the area in which heavy war materiel, tanks etc., could be deployed. *Freikorps Danmark* had to be moved from west of Biakowo to Bol. Dubowizy. The Russians had deployed large forces to try to break through to the '*Rullebanen*', to paralyse the German traffic in the area. *Freikorps Danmark* was deployed to take the village of Bol. Dubowizy on 6 June 1942. They succeeded with just a few casualties, and retired to a position of rest. The units of the German *Wehrmacht* who were defending the village quickly had to abandon it following fierce Russian attacks. Once again, the *Freikorps* was charged with taking the village on 11 June. However, this turned into a disaster, which resulted in many killed and wounded Danish soldiers. Among the dead was the new commander, Von Lettow-Vorbeck, a German. After the failed attack by *Freikorps Danmark*, Bol. Dubowizy was controlled by the Russians.

War cemetery in Korpowo

Before we drove to Bol. Dubowizy, we took a detour to the huge German war cemetery in Korpowo, which lies about 10km south of Vasilevschina. About 30,000 German soldiers are buried at the cemetery, along with some soldiers of *Freikorps Danmark*. Magnus Moeller walked around and read the memorial plates, looking for fallen comrades from the the Second World War, more than 70 years ago. There were the names of many Danes who are buried at the cemetery.

Bol. Dubowizy

Following this, we continued to the area in which the village of Bol. Dubowizy lay more than 70 years ago. Sergej, our guide, led us to the area in which *Freikorps Danmark* had their positions and trenches. It is clearly not a place many people visit. Helmets, boots and other war debris are strewn across the area. Magnus could remember a bit about the place, but the area was overgrown, as it has been more or less deserted after the end of the war in 1945. We spent some hours at this fascinating area before we returned to our hotel. An exciting historical trip was nearing its end.

Magnus Moeller, a veteran of *Freikorps Danmark*, looking for memorials to his fallen comrades. (Photo: Bax Lindhardt)

The location of Bol. Dubowizy in 1942. Today, almost nothing remains of the village. (Photo: Private)

The remains of an old position of *Freikorps Danmark*, a little west of Bol. Dubowizy. (Photo: Private)

Lars (on the left) found some German cartridge cases at Bol. Dubowizy. (Photo: Private)

Travelling home

We left the hotel in Staraya Russa and headed back to the airport in St Petersburg. However, as we had plenty of time, we visited the small village of Vitino, which lies about 30km west of the city. In January 1944, several hundred Danish soldiers were killed while fighting as part of *SS Regiment 24 Denmark*, which had been established following the abolition of *Freikorps Danmark* in 1943. Many of those who fell in the village were former volunteer soldiers of the *Freikorps*, but that is another story. We departed from Russia without any problems, but it had been a tough trip for all of us, especially for Magnus Moeller. We headed towards his home in Vejle, and returned him in good condition following the trip back to the Eastern Front. He seemed emotional that he had got a chance to once again see the places in Russia where he fought for Adolf Hitler in 1942. For the rest of us, it had been an exciting experience to see the locations where the "hated" *Freikorps Danmark* fought fierce battles during that summer.

Appendix IV

The story of Laurits Jensen, a soldier of Free Corps Denmark

Laurits Jensen. (Photo: Private)

Laurits Jensen

Born on 23 February 1922 in Loekken, Denmark.
1st Company of *Freikorps Danmark*.
Rank: *Sturmmann*.
Died on 25 December 1942.
Graveyard: Kondratowo, Russia.

Lars Larsen recounts

As can be read in the previous chapter, the two authors of this book went on a trip to Russia in 2014 with Magnus Moeller, a former soldier of *Freikorps Danmark*. On that trip, Lars Larsen acquired a *Freikorps Danmark* dog tag. Here is the story of a young Danish man who chose sides during the Second World War, a decision that he paid for with his life in a meaningless war:

> "Do you use something in your coffee?" the old woman asks me.
> "No thank you," I quickly reply.

Lars Larsen with the dog tag of Laurits Jensen. (Photo: Henning Bagger)

Don't you hold back, she tells me, and points to some homemade brown cake. The weather is suitable for coffee and brown cake. It is a grey day at the start of December 2014, and it is a bit of a coincidence that I have made contact with the old woman. I have to talk to her about something that happened 73 years before. However, first I would like to turn back time a little, not 73 years, merely two months. Finally, a long-expected trip to the Demyansk Pocket in Russia had been arranged. Visa, plane tickets, car rental etc. was all taken care of, and the day had finally arrived when we could see the location where *Freikorps Danmark* had fought so fiercely during the summer of 1942. The plane had only just landed at St Petersburg airport, when I met my Russian contact, a man in his early forties whom I have known for the last 15 years. Before I set off, he contacted me and told me that he had a *Freikorps Danmark* dog tag, which had been found in the Demyansk Pocket. We agreed to meet outside the hall of the airport, so I could see the dog tag. First, I was greeted by the Russian cold, then my contact. We quickly settled a deal, and half an hour later we left the airport, heading for Staraja Russa, about 350km further south into Russia.

Back to Denmark

When I returned from Russia, an investigation awaited me: was it possible to find the name of the soldier who matched the number on the dog tag? I went through my list of casualties of the battles of *Freikorps Danmark*, while also contacting the German authorities. In the middle of November, I succeeded in finding a matching soldier, Laurits Jensen, who had been in the battles in the Demyansk Pocket in 1942. The problem was, however, that he did not die there. Following a mail correspondence back and forth with the German authorities, the tag was confirmed to belong to the name, which I had found myself. The list of casualties also contained the names of the deceased's parents. I then wrote to the archive of local history in Loekken, and asked if they knew anything of the family. They did not, but through the census, they found that they had moved shortly after Laurits had been born. I found out that the family had moved to Arentsminde, which is located between the towns of Brovst and Aabybro in Denmark. I sent a letter to the archive of local history in Arentsminde, describing the situation, and a couple of days later I received a reply. A volunteer at the archive knew the sister of the deceased, so I got her phone number and contacted her. She was surprised to find that I had something which had belonged to her brother. But let us get back to the coffee and well-baked brown cakes, over which we talked about her brother.

Laurits Jensen

Laurits Jensen was born on 23 February 1922 in Loekken, Denmark, the oldest of three siblings. Shortly after his birth, the whole family moved to Arentsminde. When he was young, Laurits Jensen worked at a farm, where he got to know another worker, Svend Larsen. Svend was 18 months older, and had tried to join the Danish Finland Battalion in 1940, but he never made it, as the armistice between Finland and Russia was signed on 13 March 1940. Svend Larsen was among the first who joined *Freikorps Danmark* in July 1941. There is no doubt that the two young Danish men discussed the world situation on the farm in 1941.

Laurits Jensen volunteers

Laurits Jensen joined *Freikorps Danmark* at the beginning of December in 1941. He bound himself to a two-year contract, which expired on 13 December 1943, as he attended a military examination on 13 December 1941. On 8 January 1942, he travelled through Gedser to the *SS* introductory school in Sennheim, Germany. On 15 February, he finished at the school and was transferred to *Freikorps Danmark*, which was being trained in Treskau. Laurits initially became a part of the Replacement Company, then in April 1942 joined *Obersturmführer* Per Soerensen's 1st Company. He was there from the beginning when *Freikorps Danmark* was flown into the Demyansk Pocket in Russia on 7-8 May 1942. *Schütze* (Rifleman) Laurits Jensen participated in one of the major attacks by *Freikorps Danmark* on 28 May at the village of Ssutoki. A couple of days previously, on the night of 25-26 May, a patrol from *Freikorps Danmark* had observed Russian troops at the village of Ssutoki, constructing a bridgehead north of the Robja stream. The patrol also discovered that the Russians had already built bunkers and positions. In other words, the bridgehead was almost ready for the Russians to launch an attack. If the Russians did attack, *Freikorps Danmark* could lose the '*Rullebanen*',

Svend Larsen. (Photo: Frants Jensen Langhoff)

which was only 2km away from the new Russian positions. It would be a disaster for the whole Demyansk Pocket if the '*Rullebanen*' was lost to the Russians, as it was the only supply route for the trapped Germans forces. The patrol returned to its own positions early on the morning of 27 May, and quickly reported to *Hauptsturmführer* Poul Neergaard Jacobsen, commander of the 3rd Company of *Freikorps Danmark*. He immediately informed C.F. von Schalburg, the commander of *Freikorps Danmark*. The situation was then quickly discussed by von Schalburg, K.B. Martinsen and the other three company commanders, Per Soerensen of 1st Company, Boy Hansen (a German) of 2nd Company and 3rd Company's Jacobsen.

Attacking the Russians

Von Schalburg preferred to make a direct attack against the Russian bridgehead, whereas Martinsen believed that was a risky manoeuvre, without even knowing the consequences of such a move. In the end, units of 1st Company were to observe the Russians and eventually attack the bridgehead. *Untersturmführer* Johannes Just Nielsen of 1st Company, 2nd Platoon, was chosen to lead the mission. During 27 May, he chose his men for the mission. Nielsen was to advance on the eastern side, with *Oberscharführer* Anton Kern, a German, on the west. Von Schalburg and Martinsen discussed tactics and agreed that the units should get as close to the Russian positions as possible, after which they should quickly withdraw. If they had the opportunity, they should neutralise the Russian forces. The pioneer platoon of the *Freikorps* had made some special explosive charges in pipes, and the patrol was handed extra grenades and ammunition. The operation had a good start. Nielsen's group sneaked all the way up to the Russian positions without being detected, and he estimated that an attack was possible. The assault was launched, with many grenades thrown at the Russian positions, which shortly thereafter were captured by *Freikorps Danmark*, who entered the trenches and quickly overcame all the defenders. The attack was a major success for the Danish volunteers, with about 100 Russians killed. *Untersturmführer* Nielsen then ordered a retreat, but shortly thereafter the positions were bombed by 120mm mortars. The barrage lasted about 10 minutes, after which they were shot at by heavy Russian machine guns. The soldiers of *Freikorps Danmark* crawled out of the positions and quickly withdrew. Nielsen was about to be one of the last to leave when he was shot by a volley from a Russian machine gun. He fell dead in the Robja stream, where his comrades could not retrieve his body. His remains are most likely still at that location to this day. *Rottenführer* Gunner Jensen was also killed on that day, while five other members of the corps were wounded.

The Iron Cross and a wound

The Danes' success was short-lived, as the Russians reoccupied the positions during the morning of 28 May. Laurits Jensen participated in this action, and along with 18 other soldiers of *Freikorps Danmark* he received the Iron Cross 2nd Class for his efforts. On 1 June, Jensen was promoted to *Sturmmann*. The majority of the Danish volunteers who participated in the battles in the Demyansk Pocket were wounded at some point. Shrapnel from a grenade hit Jensen in his shoulder: it later had to be surgically removed. I have not managed to discover when he was wounded, but during the leave of absence in the autumn of 1942, he gave the shrapnel to his sister as a souvenir: for many years, the family had the shrapnel on display. In addition, it is certain that during the leave of absence in 1942, he went to a photographer and got a fine portrait picture, which shows a normal young man of that period, with nicely combed hair and fine clothes. His sister has still got the tie which he wore in the picture.

Home for a leave of absence

Freikorps Danmark was withdrawn from the battles at Demyansk in August 1942 and then sent home on leave. The leave soon became a disaster. They may have been praised at the start, when their special train arrived at *Godsbanegaarden* in Copenhagen on 8 September. Afterwards, however, the festivities came to a halt, and the rest of the tour across Copenhagen was particularly tense. For Laurits Jensen, his leave of absence was calm, but he could not let go of the war. He brought home a difficult task from the Demyansk Pocket. During the tough battles on 2 June, in which *Freikorps Danmark* had to move the frontline 150 metres closer to the Russian positions, many of the Danish soldiers were killed. Among them was Peder Moerch Pedersen of 1st Company, a comrade of Laurits Jensen. Jensen had the dreaded task of informing Pedersen's family, who lived in the village of Vrensted, about 32km from Arentsminde, about the death of their son on the Eastern Front. During his visit to see the parents, Jensen fell in love with Pedersen's sister. The sister also loved Jensen, and during his brief leave of absence in Denmark, they became engaged to be married. The parents were excited about this, but at the same time sad due to the information Jensen brought them about their son.

Peder Moerch Pedersen, whose sister Laurits Jensen fell in love with during his leave of absence. (Photo: Private)

Back to the Eastern Front

Leave ended on 13 October for Laurits Jensen and the rest of *Freikorps Danmark*. On 10 November, Jensen joined the DNSAP of Frits Clausen as member number 48,651. A new front awaited, which was a big contrast to that during the summer of 1942: this was winter war against the Russians. *Freikorps Danmark* had been assigned to 1st *SS*-Brigade, and at first they were supposed to fight and eliminate partisans. Instead, the Danes were placed at a part of the front where a major Russian attack was expected. Christmas Eve 1942 had a calm start, and the Russians knew that the Germans in particular would like this to be a time of quiet. The Christmas mail from Denmark had been distributed among the companies, the bunkers were decorated and the wooden ovens provided warmth in the cold Russian winter. K.B. Martinsen, commander of *Freikorps Danmark*, along with his adjutant, *Obersturmführer* Knud Thorgils, had visited the companies and wished the soldiers a merry Christmas. However, Martinsen was worried, as he expected a major Russian attack, and it did not improve the situation that he was located at the HQ of *Freikorps Danmark*, as he could not be informed about a possible Russian attack. He had forbidden the men to drink the Christmas spirits which had been handed out to them, as they should be prepared for a major Russian attack. At 5:00 p.m., Martinsen and Thorgils started their visit to the soldiers at the watch posts and the companies. As the men were very chatty, things took a little longer than planned. By 10:00 p.m., they were back at the HQ, where they could finally enjoy some Christmas dinner which the creative chefs of the *Freikorps* served, including a slaughtered pig, which provided them with some good Christmas roasts. The HQ had been decorated with the *Dannebrog* flag and leaves of spruce to try to create a little Christmas spirit.

Vagn Oest. (Photo: Peter Nybye Oest)

Laurits Jensen is killed

Things were not quiet for long, however, as the alarm sounded about 11:00 p.m. as large Russian forces launched an attack. Russian infantry, consisting of 200-300 men, attacked the left flank of *Freikorps Danmark*, which was also the location of a unit of 21st *Luftwaffe-Felddivision*. This unit was quickly overrun by the Russians, and 1st Company of *Freikorps Danmark* was left trapped in their position. Tough battles raged, in particular at the towns of Kondratowo and Laskaturina. There was hand-to-hand combat with fists and bayonets. The 4th Company of *Freikorps Danmark* was in a withdrawn position, compared to the other companies, and the Russians quickly breached the positions of 1st Company. This meant that 4th Company could not provide artillery support, without risking hitting their own soldiers. *Obersturmführer* Bent Worsoe Larsen's 2nd Company had installed themselves in a barn, where they had been celebrating Christmas. Larsen was ordered to aid 1st Company as quickly as possible. Vagn Oest, a telephone operator of 1st Company, had hidden himself in the ruins of a bombed house. From here, he could report on the exact artillery targets to 4th Company. The Russians had neutralised all the soldiers of the *Freikorps*, who were in the ruins, except Vagn Oest, who had the only telephone connection that worked. Shortly thereafter, the positions were shelled at the same time 2nd Company got there. The battle continued throughout the night, until the Russians were defeated at 6:00 a.m. on Christmas Day. A couple of hours later, the Russians launched a major attack. However, the Danish volunteers were far better prepared this time, but the Russians still took the outskirts of Kondratowo. It was not until 26 December that the remains of 1st Company could be withdrawn to safe positions. *Sturmmann* Laurits Jensen was killed on Christmas Day, receiving several shots in the chest; 15 other soldiers of *Freikorps Danmark* also fell. His death in Kondratowo ends the story of Laurits Jensen. After a couple of hours in a good company with his sister, it was time to travel back home to Randers at the end of an interesting day in the name of history.

The grave of Laurits Jensen in Kondratowo, Russia, 1943. (Photo: Private)

Appendix V

Supplementary Materials

Supplement to Chapter 5 – Velikije Luki

Danish war crimes in Bobruisk?

While the four companies and staff of officers of *Freikorps Danmark* were sent to the front, the *Freikorps*' Replacement Company stayed behind in the town of Bobruisk. Further training of the newly arrived volunteers took place here. However, some of the new soldiers had been ordered to guard a nearby camp for Jewish K.Z. prisoners. Nobody knows how many Danes guarded the camp, and if they took part in crimes against the Jewish prisoners. It is still an unanswered question, even after 70 years.

In July 2015, the Simon Wiesenthal Center reported a 90-year-old Dane to the police for crimes committed during the Second World War at Bobruisk in Belarus, where the majority of the Jewish prisoners worked themselves to death, were shot or died due to the miserable conditions. "We have found several people who had been stationed at Bobruisk, and due to their date of birth, we believe that several of them are still alive," says Efraim Zuroff of the Simon Wiesenthal Center.

As of March 2016, it was still unclear if the claims would lead to indictments against those involved.

The Commander of *Freikorps Danmark*, K.B. Martinsen, greets soldiers of the *Freikorps*' Replacement Company in Bobruisk, 1943. (Photo: Private)

The second commander of *Freikorps Danmark*, C.F. von Schalburg. (Photo: Private)

The first commander of *Freikorps Danmark*, C.P. Kryssing, as a 17-year-old in 1908. (Photo: Jann Hornum)

C.P. Kryssing as an officer of the Danish Army in 1936. (Photo: Jann Hornum)

The first Commander of *Freikorps Danmark*, C.P. Kryssing, with his family, while all was peaceful in Denmark. A few years later, both sons had died on the battlefields of the Eastern Front, and his wife had been severely injured as a German front-line nurse in Tallin, Estonia. She was disabled for the rest of her life. (Photo: Jann Hornum)

A picture of C.P. Kryssing before the war: a war which would cost him everything. (Photo: Jann Hornum)

References and sources

Per Beck Nielsen – Photo.

Statsbiblioteket (State Library) in Aarhus – Death announcements.

Danish National Museum.

Magnus Moeller's 2008 book *I krig for Danmark* (*Fighting for Denmark*).

Henning Bagger – Photo.

Knud Guldhammer Kristensen – Photo.

Bruno Mejlholm – Photo.

Bogans Forlag – Photo.

Lasse Larsen – Drawings.

Anonymous soldier of *Freikorps Danmark* – Photo.

Peter Nybye Oest – Photo.

Bax Lindhardt – Photo.

Frants Jensen Langhoff – Photo.

Special thanks to:

Jann Hornum – Photo.

Henrik Asferg Kristensen – Photo.

Poul Christensen – Photo.

Magnus Moeller – Photo.

Rigborg Dahl Nielsen – Photo.

Finn Andersen – Information.

Hanne Lillie – Information.

Inna Vinogradova – Interpreter.

John Kjaer – Translation.

Epilogue

War around our world, whether old or contemporary, has never had any winners. Humanity loses every time.

"The Commander of *Freikorps Danmark*, C.F. von Schalburg, once said: 'The war is grand and lovely.' I did not agree! The war was filthy, brutal, merciless and stinking of blood, shit, sulphur and rotting corpses. The war was crazy, [full of] pain, suffering and oceans of tears for the dead, living and wounded. The war was the breeding ground for hate, cruelty and a concentration of humanity's lowest instincts in a reflection of bestial madness," a surviving Danish soldier of *Freikorps Danmark* said after the battles on the Eastern Front.

For many of the volunteering Danish *SS* soldiers, the dream of a new Europe ended in a coffin on the Eastern Front. Many more of them are still recorded as missing. (Photo: Private)